McGraw-Hill's

TABE

Tests of Adult Basic Education

Level A

Verbal Workbook

McGraw-Hill's
TABE

Tests of Adult Basic Education

Level A
Verbal Workbook

Phyllis Dutwin, M.A.

Linda Eve Diamond

New York Chicago San Francisco Lisbon London Madrid
Mexico City Milan New Delhi San Juan Seoul Singapore
Sydney Toronto

2 3 4 5 6 7 8 9 10 11 12 13 14 15 16 QDB/QDB 12 11 10

ISBN 978-0-07-148262-2
MHID 0-07-148262-8

CONTENTS

HOW TO USE THIS BOOK

The TABE (Tests of Adult Basic Education) tests cover basic skills that you use in your everyday life. You may be surprised to find that you know more than you think you do. You may also be surprised to discover skill gaps you did not know about.

Learning how to succeed in test-taking situations makes good career sense. You will be expected to take tests throughout your adult life, both on and off the job. Standardized tests are everywhere you look: drivers' licenses, technical certification, educational placement, financial aid qualifying, job placement, and advancement exams. *TABE: Level A Verbal Workbook* is all about helping you target and master the skills you need to succeed, both on the TABE and in future situations as a lifelong learner.

Before You Begin

Before you begin to use this book, take some time to explore it. The book offers much more than question-and-answer material. Read the Table of Contents. As you browse through the book, notice the following:

- Pretest beginning each section
- Skill building in every subject
- Study Tips
- Posttests

All of these elements give you a process, or way of learning. In fact, because each section builds skills, you should read and do all the practices in order.

What if you think you have great strength in one of the subjects? Take the Skills Assessment for that subject anyway. Even if your answers are almost all correct. You should still review this section. Of course, be sure to take all of the post tests.

One section, "Spelling," needs a special comment. *You should not study this section straight through* from first page to last. Correct spelling is best learned slowly and through repetition. Take the spelling pretest early in the process. If you find that spelling is not your strong subject, start the section. No matter what else you are working on, study a *small* part of the spelling section at the same time. If you use the tips provided and study consistently, you can improve your spelling.

Use This Book as Your Personal Trainer

Step 1: Develop a fitness plan.
- Complete Section 1, "Work Smarter, Not Harder."

Step 2: Warm up.
- Target skills you need to strengthen.
- Take the pretest for each section before reading.

Step 3: Work out.
- Read instructions for each skill.
- Pace yourself through the practices.
- Take the posttest for each section.
- Go back to review when needed.

STUDY TIP: PRETESTS

Do *not* study for the skills pretests that begin each subject section. The results of each assessment will help you:

- Compare what you already know with what you *need* to know.
- Make a learning plan for choosing and using the lessons that follow.
- See your progress as you work through the practices and see how much you have learned by the time you complete the posttest.

STUDY TIP: POSTTESTS

Set aside concentrated time to take each posttest. Treat them as though they were actual TABE tests. Your best indication of how much you learned will come from working through the posttests without distractions or interruptions. This will help you learn which skills, if any, you need to go back and review. As you work through the book, it is useful to pace yourself through skill-building explanations and practices, allowing yourself to flip back to an explanation that will help you better understand the skill. However, the posttest will only be an accurate test of what you have learned and what areas need more study time if you work straight through, without looking back at explanations.

ABOUT THE AUTHORS

Phyllis Dutwin is President of Dutwin Associates, a company that consults with major publishers to develop books for adult students. Her Web address is http://PhyllisDutwin.com.

Linda Eve Diamond comes from a corporate training background and is the author of several business, educational, and self-help books. Her Web address is http://LindaEveDiamond.com.

McGraw-Hill's

TABE

Tests of Adult Basic Education

Level A

Verbal Workbook

Work Smarter, Not Harder

LESSON 1 **Identify Your Target**

Goal setting and timelines are important for your success. This chapter is a shortened version of Section 1 in the original TABE Level A book. If you completed this section in the original book, think about whether your goals or time frames have changed. You may want to fill it out again. If you did not consider these questions before now, take some time to complete this section. Not being clear about your goals and how to reach them will make you work harder in the end; work smarter, not harder.

Where Are You Headed?

If you did not take the time to think about your goals in the original TABE Level A book, think about them now.

My Goals

I am studying to improve my basic academic skills to:
- [ ] Enroll in an associate degree program.
- [ ] Enter a vocational certificate program.
- [ ] Obtain admission to a job training program.
- [ ] Obtain admission to a career advancement program.
- [ ] Qualify for a promotion at my workplace.
- [ ] Qualify for certification in _____.
- [ ] Complete graduation requirements for _____.
- [ ] Successfully exit the Welfare to Work program.
- [ ] Become more independent in handling my affairs.
- [ ] Gain personal satisfaction.
- [ ] Help family members with their schooling.
- [ ] _____
- [ ] _____
- [ ] _____

After I upgrade my skills and score well on the TABE, I plan to

_____

_____

_____ .

A vision I have for my future is

_____

_____

_____ .

When Do You Want to Get There?

Today's date: _____

I want to take the TABE Level A test by this date: _____

What's the Score?

Programs vary in their TABE score requirements. Take time to contact your program supervisor to clarify what the TABE score requirements are for what you want to do.

Look at the TABE scores required for admission into the following programs of study at one community college:

Program of Study	Pre-enrollment TABE Test Scores		
	Reading	Math	Language
Accounting	9.0	10.0	9.0
Wireless Communications	10.0	10.0	10.0
Marketing	9.0	9.0	9.0

The program I wish to enter or exit after taking the TABE requires me to achieve a minimum score of: _____ Reading _____ Language _____ Math _____ Spelling

What Do You Need to Succeed as a Test Taker?

Reflection: Past Experiences with Tests

The last time I took a standardized test was _____.

My results were: _____ Excellent _____ Good _____ OK _____ A Disaster

I think my performance on that test was due to_____
_____.

In general, I consider myself a _____ Good _____ Fair _____ Poor test taker.

My biggest problem with taking tests is _____.

I think I need to _____.

Test-Taking Strategies

I am familiar with, and am able to put into practice, the following test-taking strategies. I know how to

• Visualize success for self-confidence and best results.	Yes	No	Need practice
• Prepare physically for the test day.	Yes	No	Need practice
• Identify key words in questions and directions.	Yes	No	Need practice
• Recognize pitfalls of multiple-choice tests.	Yes	No	Need practice
• Use process of elimination to check multiple-choice questions.	Yes	No	Need practice
• Relax by using breathing techniques.	Yes	No	Need practice
• Take one-minute breaks to relieve stress during the test.	Yes	No	Need practice
• Pace myself during the test to finish within the time limit.	Yes	No	Need practice
• Know when to leave a question that is giving me trouble.	Yes	No	Need practice
• Use time that is left at the end to check my work.	Yes	No	Need practice

LESSON 2 Analyze Yourself as a Learner

Self-Assessment and Planning

In this section you will take steps to better understand yourself as a learner. You also need to examine and manage the time you have to prepare for the TABE. In addition, you will be able to identify, understand, and develop strategies to overcome the barriers that many adults face as learners. The result will be a plan of action that will help you target success.

What Kind of a Learner Are You?

Because people learn in different ways, it is important for you to understand how *you* learn best. This information will help you develop a learning plan that will target success on the TABE and enhance your other learning goals.

Complete the Learner Preference Worksheet below to help you better understand how *you* prefer to learn.

Learner Preference Worksheet

1. *What time(s) of day or night do you feel better able to study/work/read/write?*
   Early morning _____   Afternoon _____
   Early evening _____   Late night _____

2. *Do you prefer to study or learn by yourself or with others?*
   I like learning about new things with a study group. _____
   I like learning about new things by myself. _____
   I like learning something new with one other person to help me. _____

3. *Do you learn best by:*
   Reading about something? _____
   Seeing a picture or graph? _____
   Hearing someone explain something? _____
   Practicing what I'm learning about? _____
   Writing it down? _____
   Talking about it with someone else? _____

4. *What length of time do you prefer to spend studying?*
   I prefer to work for periods of two hours or more. _____
   I prefer to work for shorter periods of time (less than an hour). _____
   I can work whenever time permits. _____

5. *How's your concentration?*
   I need complete silence when I study or read. _____
   I can study or read with some background noise. _____
   I can study or read in any environment, quiet or noisy. _____

Examine the items you have checked above to get a picture of how you learn best. Use this information to fill in your Learner Preference Statement:

Learner Preference Statement

I prefer to study in the (1) _____ with (2) _____ .

I learn best by (3) _____ .

I prefer to spend (4) _____ studying.

I study best with (5) _____ .

We will use the above information to develop your Personal Learning Plan later in this chapter. You have thought about how you learn and study best. Now you should be aware of, and plan for, obstacles that might get in the way of your success.

What Are Your Barriers?

We are all faced with a variety of life issues and challenges that can, if we let them, sabotage our success. These barriers can be overcome if we are aware of the supports that we can draw upon to help us with them.

You can categorize barriers in three ways: institutional, circumstantial, and personal. Read this discussion of barriers. An exercise will follow to help you plan for and overcome some of these barriers to your success.

Institutional barriers are those over which we have no control. They are put in place by a school, program, or a class. Institutional barriers can include inconvenient class times, difficult registration procedures, financial aid deadlines, and other things that keep us from taking a class or continuing with one. These barriers may cause difficulties, but can often be worked around. (For example, you could change other schedules or find help with complicated processes or tight deadlines.)

Circumstantial barriers are difficult, but are more often within our control. These barriers may include lack of time, money, child care, or transportation. They can make it difficult for us to reach our learning goals. However, setting goals and priorities will help you find a way around circumstantial barriers.

Personal barriers are mainly in our control, yet they are typically the most difficult to overcome. They include long-held beliefs about our abilities as a learner or student.

Personal barriers include:

- Feelings of being too old to take classes or to learn.
- Feelings that we are not smart enough to do well in class, or even in one particular subject. (Many people have a fear of math and feel they cannot do well in that subject, but find they do well in it once they let go of those fears and focus on learning.)
- Negative feelings about school or learning because of poor experiences with school earlier in life.

These barriers may keep some people from even attempting to go back to school or to take a course. They might also be the cause of someone dropping out of a class or program. The good news is that there are ways to deal with, and overcome, many of these barriers.

Identify Your Support Systems

Many sources of support exist for you. Identify these within your own family, within your circle of friends, and within your neighborhood and community.

Family—Try to identify people within your close or extended family whom you can ask for help if you need to. Ask yourself these questions:

1. Do I have a parent, sibling, aunt, uncle, or anyone who can provide child care, even on a short-term basis, so I can study, go to the library, or go to a class?

   I can ask _____.

   I can ask _____.

2. Is there anyone in my family whom I can call on short notice to help me with transportation or financial needs?

   I can call _____.

   I can call _____.

Friends—Identify friends, also, who might be able to help you with child care, studying, or a ride if you need one. Are there things you can offer to do for them in exchange? Can you offer them child care or other support at times when they need it? Sometimes, friends set up an informal child-care exchange program where they develop a schedule of support for each other.

I will ask my friend _____ for help with _____.

In exchange, I can offer _____.

I will ask my friend _____ for help with _____.

In exchange, I can offer _____.

Neighbors—Do you have any neighbors who might consider helping you on short notice if you need it?

A neighbor I might call on for help is _____.

Another neighbor I might call on for help is _____.

Community—Many social services are available in the community to assist you if you need them. These services include child care, transportation, clothing, food, shelter, financial aid, and counseling. Find community service telephone numbers online or in the front of your telephone book. Many communities offer:

- Health centers
- Family services
- Educational financial aid services

I will seek out these community services:

_____

_____

_____

_____

_____

_____

Fill out the Balancing Barriers and Supports Worksheet using the two steps outlined below.

1. List the *Institutional, Circumstantial, and Personal* barriers you might face. Use the descriptions on page 5 to help you identify the different barriers. Write these in the spaces provided on the left side of the form below.
2. List your barriers below in the left-hand column. Match each barrier with people (friends, family, neighbors) or community services that might help you overcome each one. List those "supports" in the right-hand column.

Balancing Barriers and Supports Worksheet

Barriers	Supports
Institutional	
Circumstantial	
Personal	
Notes to Myself	

Make Time for Learning

A common complaint of adult learners is that they lack time for studying and other learning activities. This section will help you document and analyze how you currently spend your time. It will help you develop a plan to include your learning activities.

Step One: Look at this weeklong calendar. Place an *X* through the times when you know you have fixed activities, such as job hours, family meal times, and other schedules that cannot be changed. (If your study hours extend beyond this calendar, correct the one below or create your own.)

My Weekly Schedule

	Mon	Tues	Wed	Thurs	Fri	Sat	Sun
6 A.M.							
7 A.M.							
8 A.M.							
9 A.M.							
10 A.M.							
11 A.M.							
12 P.M.							
1 P.M.							
2 P.M.							
3 P.M.							
4 P.M.							
5 P.M.							
6 P.M.							
7 P.M.							
8 P.M.							
9 P.M.							
10 P.M.							
11 P.M.							
12 A.M.							

Step Two: You have identified time slots that are *not* available for learning. Now ask yourself the critical questions below to help you plan your best times for learning during the week. Use the information you recorded about yourself on the Learner Preference Statement, page 5, to help you.

Step Three: Complete the following statement:

I will dedicate _____ hours every day (or _____ hours every week) to studying for this test.

Make a commitment that fits into your schedule. If you put down more hours of study than you will have time for, you will set yourself up to fail. Set yourself up for success instead. Write down a reasonable number of hours and stick to it. If you fall short of that goal, just keep doing the best you can. The goal is only to help you stay on track with your studies, not to discourage you if you fall behind.

Use the answers to the questions below to help identify the best times for you to study. If there is a conflict, use your Balancing Barriers and Supports Worksheet to help you identify your supports.

When do I learn best? _____

_____

How much time do I need during the day or week to study?

_____

_____

Are there any times available when I will be able to study without interruption?

_____

_____

Make time in your schedule for studying by calling on your supports for help with tasks that must be done daily or weekly. Write these times on your calendar above and on the lines below:

_____

_____

_____

_____

LESSON 3 Put It to Work: Here's How

Create a Personal Learning Plan

Now that you have reflected on your situation, put the information to work for you. Complete this learning plan as directed. Next, photocopy it, and put it in a place where you will see it every day.

My Learning Plan

Goal/s: (page 1) _____

_____

_____

Things I need to do to reach my goals: _____

_____

_____

My Promises

I will study at the times, and in the ways, I learn best.
Write your Learner Preference Statement here: (page 5)

I will refer often to my Balancing Barriers and Supports Worksheet. (page 7)
I will continue to try to find and use the supports I need to overcome obstacles.
I will consult my weekly calendar (page 8) and use the study time I have scheduled.

I WILL SUCCEED.

LESSON 1 **Getting Started**

Following is a shortened version of the Lesson 1 reading questions in the original TABE Level A book. If you completed this section in the original book, think about whether your answers have changed. You may want to fill it out again. If you did not fill it out before, take some time now to complete this section.

Reflection: Reading in My Daily Life

I read approximately ___ hrs a day / ___ hrs a week to keep informed of current events and other issues that concern me.

I read approximately ___ hrs a day / ___ hrs a week for workplace tasks.

I enjoy reading _____.

I would like to improve my ability to read _____.

Comprehension

I am able to understand, analyze, and use these types of materials:

Newspapers	____ Yes	____ No	____ Need practice	____ Don't know
Instructions	____ Yes	____ No	____ Need practice	____ Don't know
Maps, charts, and graphs	____ Yes	____ No	____ Need practice	____ Don't know
Stories and novels	____ Yes	____ No	____ Need practice	____ Don't know
Business letters	____ Yes	____ No	____ Need practice	____ Don't know
Manuals, handbooks	____ Yes	____ No	____ Need practice	____ Don't know
Standardized forms	____ Yes	____ No	____ Need practice	____ Don't know
Indexes, tables of contents	____ Yes	____ No	____ Need Practice	____ Don't know

Vocabulary Knowledge

I know how to figure out the meaning of a word from its *context* (the way it is used in a passage).

_____ Yes _____ No _____ Need practice _____ Don't know

I know how to identify the meaning of a word by analyzing its *structure* (roots, prefixes, and suffixes).

_____ Yes _____ No _____ Need practice _____ Don't know

Reading Skills Pretest

Read this article on screen time and then answer questions 1–7.

Screen Time

How many times have you said this (or heard it): "Turn off the TV. It's a school night. Do your homework." Now you can feel good about giving that command since studies confirm that children do worse in school if they watch TV and play video games during the school week.

Recent studies gave us an additional fact: R-rated movies have a negative effect on learning. Interestingly, researchers think that R-rated movies make boys more aggressive. Aggression may lead to poor school performance.

What is your daily screen time, or time spent looking at TV or DVD's, the computer, or playing video games? Experts agree that if you spend under two hours a day, you're not doing badly. More than that indicates a need for change.

And what will you do with time that you gain by reducing screen time? Obviously, you'll have more time for family, for conversation, for relating to people around you. In addition, leaving the screen helps you to keep more physically active, a definite help in the fight against weight gain.

At the very least, we can all—parents or not—use some rules that will help us and our families to use our screens wisely. Perhaps the family can decide that no one will go over the two-hour mark. You can reduce the temptation by removing TVs, computers, and video games from bedrooms and the kitchen. Another interesting finding is that families that eat together are happier families.

1. The main idea of this passage is that
   A Only boys need to reduce screen time.
   B We may spend a lot of time watching TV, but no one thinks that is a bad thing.
   C We all need to reduce screen time to increase learning power and good health.
   D No matter how much a child watches TV and plays video games, he or she will be a good reader.

2. You can infer from this passage that the author wants
   A Us to drop the subject.
   B Parents to limit their screen time, too.
   C Children to increase their time at the computer.
   D Families to have a meal together once a month.

3. One solution to spending too much screen time is to
   A Never buy a TV, computer, or video game.
   B Put a TV in every room.
   C Have children go outside to play no matter how bad the weather.
   D Remove TVs from the bedrooms and the kitchen.

4. The passage states that R-rated movies make boys more *aggressive*. *Aggressive* means
   A Violent.
   B Intelligent.
   C Calm.
   D Unwilling to fight.

5. Although parents often try to enforce the two-hour rule,

    A   They rarely succeed.

    B   They don't necessarily follow it themselves.

    C   Not many people think it helps children do better in school.

    D   Dinner time always gets in the way.

6. By *screen time,* the author means

    A   Television only.

    B   Television as well as telephones.

    C   Television, computers, and video.

    D   Computers only.

7. An important concept in this passage is that too much screen time keeps us

    A   Very happy.

    B   Very physically active.

    C   Caught up with all of our work.

    D   From relating to family.

Read these two employment ads. Then answer questions 8–13.

Dental Receptionist-Secretary. Join our fast-paced pediatric dental team. Must enjoy people and like being busy. Top salary plus benefits. 5 days per week. Simple computer skills a must. Send resume to Dr. Francine Lyons, 723 King Street, Philadelphia, PA 19127.

Dental Receptionist-Scheduler. Busy general dentistry office seeks a self-starting, detail-oriented person. Top salary. Dental and computer experience a must. Send resume and cover letter to Dr. George Fuller, 909 Main St., Saunderstown, RI 02852. Or submit resume and cover letter to: G_Fuller@loa.com.

8. Both dental offices are seeking a receptionist, but one needs a _____, and the other needs a _____.

    A   Computer specialist, nurse

    B   Dentist, receptionist

    C   Secretary, scheduler

    D   Pediatric, scheduler

9. An important difference about the first office is that

    A   It is pediatric.

    B   The dentist is a woman.

    C   It is not as busy.

    D   There is no computer.

10. *Pediatric* is another way of saying

    A   High quality work.

    B   Senior citizens only.

    C   Dentistry without pain.

    D   Care of children.

11. From what you know about dentists' offices, you can conclude that a scheduler is a person who

    A   Picks up lunch.

    B   Makes appointments.

    C   Collects fees.

    D   Opens the mail and pays bills.

12. The first ad asks for a resume while the second ad asks

    A   The job seeker to set up an appointment for an interview.

    (B)   For both a resume and a cover letter.

    C   For a dental health history.

    D   The year of the reader's graduation from dental school.

13. The second ad gives the job seeker the option of sending

    (A)   A resume and cover letter to an e-mail address.

    B   A picture and cover letter via e-mail.

    C   Just a resume via e-mail.

    D   A request for an interview.

Read this passage about keeping fit at work. Then answer questions 14–18.

Work Out at Work

If you're working in an office seven to eight hours a day, you don't have much chance to move around, but you do have a good chance of injuring yourself. The question is, how do you work in a small space for a long period of time and not end up in pain? Some of the solutions have to do with what you can do physically. Other solutions are related to improving your workstation.

Staying in the same position—for example, slouching at the computer—can lead to severe upper and lower back pain. Obviously, you need to get out of that position as often as possible. First, coach yourself to tighten your abdominal muscles and sit taller. Then, remind yourself to get out of the chair at least every 20 minutes or so. You can still be productive; take a call, make a call, or organize your desk. Getting away from the computer momentarily is also a good way to prevent repetitive stress injuries. In fact, doctors say you should not type continuously for more than 10 minutes before switching to another task.

You will find that simple exercises, done at your desk, will prevent pain and raise your energy level as well. Always ask your doctor before you start any exercise or stretching routine. The following are just a few of the many that you can try:

- To relieve stress in your head and shoulders, simply roll your head clockwise and counter-clockwise.
- To stretch your lower back, stand up, bend over, and dangle your head and arms toward the floor. Be sure that you have no existing back injury that would be harmed by this particular move.
- To stretch your legs and keep circulation in them, stand up and lift up on the balls of your feet. Repeat several times.

A well-planned workstation contributes to your physical comfort. Comfort starts at your desk. Is your workspace large enough for you to be able to move, stretch, and change your position or posture? Comfort also depends upon a well-fitted chair as well as a desk that is at the right height. Fortunately, most desk or workstation chairs are adjustable. If you can't manage the adjustments yourself, ask for help!

Finally, don't forget to put the proper light on your computer and desk. If you don't, you may experience headaches, burning eyes, or blurry vision and other related problems. Optometrists suggest that desks be set up to avoid direct light on the computer screen or in your eyes. In addition, you should choose light that is neither too bright nor too dim. Current thinking is that incandescent bulbs are better than fluorescent ones for your comfort. You can easily adjust your computer monitor's contrast to avoid glare, or invest in a glare filter to do it for you. Of course, you should see an eye doctor every year to check your vision and to discuss any problems.

14. You can conclude that a main idea of this article is that workplace injuries
    A   Are inevitable.
    B   Can be related to workspace.
    C   Are only related to lighting.
    D   Both B and C above.

15. Even if you have the perfect workspace, you
    A   Need to see your eye doctor every year.
    B   Can never protect your back while sitting at the computer.
    C   Never need to ask for help.
    D   Should consider a job change yearly.

16. If you have had your eyes checked but still leave your workstation with a headache every day, you should
    A   Tell your boss you'll have to leave the company.
    B   Put a glare filter on your computer monitor.
    C   Remove fluorescent bulbs and replace them with incandescent bulbs.
    D   Both B and C above.

17. Comfort at your workstation depends on
    A   Your boss, fluorescent lighting, and your desk.
    B   Incandescent lighting, a well-fitted chair, and space to move.
    C   Your hours in the office.
    D   Your screen saver, your lunch space, and your lounge chair.

18. In paragraph 2, another word for *abdominal* is
    A   Tightening.
    B   Taller.
    C   Repetitive.
    D   Stomach.

Read this passage on the Presidential Medal of Freedom. Then answer questions 19–25.

The *Presidential Medal of Freedom* is the highest civilian award in the United States. President Harry Truman first gave this award in 1945 to honor people who served during WWII. President John F. Kennedy revived the medal and began the tradition of awarding the medal annually, on or near July 4. The award is given to several people annually. Unlike many other US awards, the Presidential Medal of Freedom can be awarded to non-US citizens.

The *Presidential Medal of Freedom* recognizes individuals who have made "an especially meritorious contribution to the security or national interests of the United States, or to world peace, or to cultural or other significant public or private endeavors."

President George W. Bush presented the Presidential Medal of Freedom to baseball legend Henry Aaron during a ceremony at the White House, July 9, 2002. This is his story.

On April 8, 1974, Hank Aaron of the Atlanta Braves hit his 715'th career home run, surpassing Babe Ruth's legendary record. However, as an African American player who had received death threats during his pursuit of one of baseball's most distinguished records, the achievement was bittersweet. Nevertheless, the largest crowd in the history of Atlanta Stadium was with him that night to cheer his accomplishment, and on June 18, he was invited to speak before the U.S. Congress.

Henry Louis Aaron, Jr., born in Mobile, Alabama, in 1934, entered the major leagues in 1954, just eight years after Jackie Robinson pioneered integrated play. Three years later, with little fanfare, Aaron was named the National League's Most Valuable Player as the Milwaukee Braves won the pennant. A few weeks later, his three home runs in the World Series helped his team triumph over the heavily favored New York Yankees. Although "Hammerin' Hank" specialized in home runs, he was also an extremely dependable batter, and by the end of his career, he held baseball's career record for most runs batted in: 2,297. In 1976, he left the playing field for the Braves' front office, where he became one of baseball's first African American executives and a leading spokesperson for minority hiring. He was inducted into the Baseball Hall of Fame in 1982.

Adapted from www.medaloffreedom.com/HankAaron.htm

19. The writer says that Aaron's homerun record was *bittersweet*. A dictionary gives the following definitions for *bittersweet*. Which does the author mean?

   A Smelling or tasting both bitter and sweet at the same time

   (B) Causing feelings of happiness and sadness at the same time

   C A poisonous climbing plant that has bright red seeds

   D A sprawling plant with purple flowers

20. An important detail about Hank Aaron's baseball skills is that

   A He only knew how to hit home runs.

   B He was a much more talented executive than he was a baseball player.

   (C) He was an extremely dependable batter.

   D He entered baseball before Jackie Robinson.

21. The author's intention was to

(A) Contrast Aaron's great talent with the great prejudice of the time.

B Give the reader all possible baseball statistics.

C Convince the reader that Aaron should not have won an award.

D Provide the reader with names of all of Aaron's teammates.

22. The first Presidential Medal of Freedom was given by

A Hank Aaron.

(B) John F. Kennedy.

C Harry Truman.

D Atlanta.

23. When did "Hammerin' Hank" surpass Babe Ruth's record?

(A) When he hit his 715'th career homerun

B The day he retired

C When he pitched for the last time

D In 1976

24. Another of Aaron's distinctions was

A Becoming a famous writer.

B Making more money than anyone has in baseball.

C Becoming the quarterback for the Patriots.

(D) Becoming one of baseball's first African American executives.

25. Jackie Robinson actually *pioneered* integrated play. In this sentence, what does *pioneered* mean?

A He was the first person to hit 715 home runs

(B) He made a long journey to California

C He was the only African American to play on a team in the 20th century

D He was the first African American to be hired by a white team

Read this article on the history of the early compass. Answer questions 26–33.

History of the Navigational Compass

The compass is considered one of the four great inventions of Ancient China. In the past, people thought that the compass was developed in the second millennium BC. However, the honor of inventing the compass belongs to the Chinese. The earliest recorded use of lodestone as a direction finder was in a fourth century BC Chinese book, *Book of the Devil Valley Master. Dream Pool Essay,* written in AD 1086 by Song Dynasty scholar Shen Kua, contained a detailed description of how a needle was magnetized by rubbing its tip with lodestone. The magnetic needle was hung with one single strain of silk with a bit of wax attached to the center of the needle.

The earliest recorded use of a compass in navigation lies in Zhu Yu's book of AD 1117. In the book he says,

"The navigator knows the geography; he watches the stars at night, watches the sun at day. When it is dark and cloudy, he watches the compass."

After this time, there is much debate about what happened to the compass. Theories include its travel to the Middle East via the Silk Road. From there it is said to have traveled to Europe, and later from Europe to the Middle East. There is also talk of the independent creation of the compass in Europe and then its transfer thereafter to the Middle East. The latter two theories are supported by evidence of the Arabic word for "Compass" (*al-konbas*) possibly being taken from the old Italian word for compass. Other evidence includes the earlier mentioning of the compass in European works rather than in Arabic ones. The first European mention of the directional compass occurs in Alexander Neckam's *On the Natures of Things*, probably written in Paris in 1190. As for the Arab world, Yemeni Sultan al-Ashraf appears to have written the earliest confirmed mention of the compass in 1290, though some authors assert an earlier recording, as early as 1242, for Arabic and 1231 for Persian.

Prior to the introduction of the compass, direction at sea was primarily determined by the position of celestial bodies. In some places, the use of soundings, line measurements of the depth, supplemented celestial navigation. Difficulties arose where the sea was too deep for soundings and conditions were continually overcast or foggy. Thus the compass was not as useful everywhere. For example, the Arabs could generally rely on clear skies in navigating the Persian Gulf and the Indian Ocean. They also made use of the predictable nature of the monsoons. This may explain in part their relatively late adoption of the compass. Mariners in the relatively shallow Baltic made extensive use of soundings.

In the Mediterranean, however, the practice from ancient times had been to curtail sea travel between October and April, due in part to the lack of dependably clear skies during the Mediterranean winter. In addition, much of the sea is too deep for soundings. With improvements in dead reckoning methods and the development of better charts, this changed during the second half of the 13th century. By around 1290 the sailing season could start in late January or February and end in December. The additional few months were of considerable economic importance; since it enabled Venetian convoys, for instance, to make two round trips a year to the eastern Mediterranean, instead of one.

Around the time Europeans learned of the compass, traffic between the Mediterranean and northern Europe increased, and one factor may be that the compass made crossing the Bay of Biscay safer and easier.

Adapted from www.wikipedia.com

26. You can conclude from paragraphs one and two that lodestone was
   A The source of magnification in the compass.
   B A way of building early ships.
   C A way to express dislike.
   D A sounding string.

27. Whether a compass was used had to do with
   A The size of the ship.
   B The development of charts.
   C The weather.
   D The year the ship was built.

28. A main idea in this passage is that the compass

    A   Was an insignificant invention.

    B   Really came into use in the 18th century.

    C   Was co-invented by an American and a European.

    D   Is considered one of the four greatest inventions of Ancient China.

29. An important detail in the passage states that before the use of the compass,

    A   No one ever traveled anywhere.

    B   Everyone was waiting for Asia to invent it.

    C   Direction at sea was mostly determined by the position of celestial bodies.

    D   Everyone waited for sunny skies and shallow water.

30. Celestial bodies are

    A   Objects we observe in the sky.

    B   Songs we hear played frequently.

    C   Beautiful people.

    D   Objects around us on earth.

31. The earliest recorded use of lodestone as a direction finder

    A   Goes back to Shen Kua in AD 1086.

    B   Goes back to the 4th century BC.

    C   Has been totally disproved.

    D   Was written in the *Book of the Devil Valley Master*.

32. According to the passage,

    A   Mediterranean skies were not dependable ever.

    B   Mediterranean skies were undependable between October and April.

    C   The best trade took place between October and April.

    D   The only trade took place between October and April.

33. Theories about the compass say that it traveled

    A   The Silk Road.

    B   From the Middle East to Europe.

    C   From Europe to the Middle East.

    D   All of the above.

Read this story, adapted from *The Cask of Amontillado,* by the first American writer of mysteries and horror stories, Edgar Allan Poe (1809–1849). Answer questions 34–41.

The thousand injuries of Fortunato I had borne as I best could, but when he ventured upon insult I vowed revenge. I must not only punish but punish with impunity. A wrong is forgiven when the avenger is responding to a greater wrong.

It must be understood that neither by word nor deed had I given Fortunato cause to doubt my good will. I continued, as was my way, to smile in his face, and he did not perceive that my smile *now* was at the thought of his suffering.

He had a weak point—this Fortunato—although in other regards he was a man to be respected and even feared. He prided himself on his knowledge of wine. In painting and jewels, Fortunato, like his Italian countrymen, was a quack, but in the matter of old wines he was sincere. In this respect I did not differ from him materially; I was skillful in the Italian wines myself, and bought largely whenever I could.

It was about dusk, one evening during the supreme madness of the carnival season, that I encountered my friend. He approached me with excessive warmth, for he had been drinking much. The man wore a multi-colored costume and a conical cap with bells.

I said to him: "My dear Fortunato, you are luckily met. How remarkably well you are looking to-day. But I have received a container of what passes for Amontillado, and I have my doubts."

"How?" he said. "Amontillado? Impossible! And in the middle of the carnival!"

"I have my doubts," I replied; "and I was silly enough to pay the full Amontillado price without consulting you in the matter. You were not to be found, and I was fearful of losing a bargain."

"Amontillado!"

"I have my doubts."

"Amontillado!"

"And I must satisfy them."

"Amontillado!"

"I am on my way to Luchresi. If anyone has a critical turn it is he. He will tell me—"

"Luchresi cannot tell Amontillado from Sherry."

"And yet some fools will say that his taste is a match for your own."

"Come, let us go."

"Where?"

"To your vaults."

"My friend, no; I will not impose upon your good nature. I perceive you have somewhere to go. Luchresi—"

"I have no engagement; come."

"My friend, no. It is not the engagement, but the severe cold with which I perceive you are afflicted. The vaults are terribly damp."

"Let us go, nevertheless. The cold is nothing. Amontillado! You have been imposed upon. And as for Luchresi, he cannot distinguish Sherry from Amontillado."

Fortunato took my arm; and putting on a mask of black silk and drawing a hooded cloak closely around me, I allowed him to hurry me to my home.

I took two lighted torches, and giving one to Fortunato, took him through several suites of rooms to the archway that led into the vaults. I passed down a long and winding staircase, requesting him to be cautious as he followed. We came at length to the foot of the descent, and stood together upon the damp ground of the catacombs . . .

The gait of my friend was unsteady, and the bells upon his cap jingled as he strode.

"The wine," he said.

"It is farther on," said I; "but observe the white web-work which gleams from these cavern walls."

He turned towards me, and looked into my eyes with two watery eyes that distilled the look of intoxication.

"Nitre?" he asked.

"Nitre," I replied. "How long have you had that cough?"

"Ugh! ugh! ugh! —ugh! ugh! ugh! —ugh! ugh! ugh! —ugh! ugh! ugh! —ugh! ugh! ugh!"

My poor friend found it impossible to reply for many minutes.

"It is nothing," he said, at last.

"Come," I said, with decision, "we will go back; your health is precious. You are rich, respected, admired, beloved; you are happy, as once I was. You are a man to be missed. For me it is no matter. We will go back; you will be ill, and I cannot be responsible. Besides, there is Luchresi—"

"Enough," he said; "the cough's a mere nothing; it will not kill me. I shall not die of a cough."

"True—true," I replied.

Adapted from *The Cask of Amontillado,* by Edgar Allan Poe

34. From the first paragraph, you can tell that this is going to be a story of

A   Great friendship.

B   Great revenge.

C   Great love.

D   Great wine.

35. In the first paragraph, to "punish with impunity" means

A   To hurt someone physically.

B   To hurt someone and not be punished for it.

C   Treat Fortunato with special kindness.

D   Punish myself for even thinking of hurting Fortunato.

36. The first sentence says, "The thousand injuries of Fortunato I had borne as best I could . . ." Why does the author use first person? ("I"—the main character is speaking directly to the reader.)

A   The author wants you to experience the speaker's feelings as strongly as possible.

B   The author wants you to feel sympathy for Fortunato.

C   The author wants you to hate the speaker.

D   All of the above.

37. From Fortunato's reaction to the name of the wine, Amontillado, you can assume that

   A   The wine was worth very little.

   B   The wine might be rare and expensive.

   C   The wine is served only during carnival.

   D   The narrator and Fortunato will become great friends.

38. You know that something terrible is going to happen when the narrator calls himself

   A   Amontillado.

   B   Fortunato.

   C   The avenger.

   D   Nitre.

39. The narrator appeals to Fortunato's vanity by saying

   A   "Luchresi cannot tell Amontillado from Brandy."

   B   "The vaults are insufficiently damp."

   C   "I was silly enough to pay the full Amontillado price without consulting you in the matter."

   D   "The cold is nothing. Amontillado!"

40. Poe uses words to build great visual contrast when he refers to

   A   Fortunato's gray costume and the vault's bright lights.

   B   The flames they carry and the bright sun.

   C   Luchesi's costume and the sherry.

   D   The dark catacombs and the jingling bells on Fortunato's cap.

41. The words, "True—true . . ." at the end of the passage make the outcome of the story clear:

   A   Fortunato and the narrator will become best friends.

   B   Fortunato will judge the wine as excellent.

   C   Fortunato and the narrator will leave the vaults arm in arm.

   D   Fortunato will not leave the vaults alive.

Answer Key: Section 2, Lesson 1 (Pretest)

1. C	2. B	3. D	4. A	5. B	6. C
✗ 7. D	8. C	9. A	10. D	11. B	12. B
13. A	✗14. B	15. A	16. D	17. B	18. D
19. B	20. C	21. A	✗22. C	23. A	24. D
✗ 25. D	26. A	27. C	28. D	29. C	30. A
31. B	✗ 32. B	✗ 33. D	34. B	35. B	36. A
37. B	✗38. C	39. C	40. D	41. D	

To discover your areas for skill improvement in the Reading Section:

1. Once you have checked your answers against the answer key, go back to compare your incorrect answers with the correct ones. Notice whether you understand why the answer given is the correct one.

2. Total your number of correct answers out of the 41 possible answers. If you had fewer than 38 correct answers, pay special attention to this chapter and be sure to take the Reading Posttest.

3. After completing the chapter, go back to review the Reading Pretest questions that you answered incorrectly to see if you have a better understanding of why the answer was incorrect.

Reading for Main Ideas

You may have noticed that this is always one of the first reading skills taught in any reading improvement course. Of course, the reason is simple. How much can we get out of reading if we're missing the main point?

A reader should prepare himself or herself for reading just as an athlete prepares for an athletic event. Athletes need to warm up before a practice session, and so does a reader before a reading session. Your warm-up involves getting your brain "warmed up" to the subject matter. How do you do that? Look first for the main idea.

STUDY TIP

- Look at the title of the passage if there is one. The title should, at least, suggest the topic. Does it give clues to the main idea?
- Ask yourself, before you read the passage, whether you already know something about the topic. You may be able to predict what it is about.
- Ask yourself what you can expect to learn from the reading. After you finish reading, go back and check to see if you were right.
- Look for graphic information and pictures for clues to the main idea *before* you start reading.
- As you read, *actively* look for the main idea.

This warm-up will take very little time. The more often you practice this skill, the faster you will become, and it is well worth it. At the end of a reading, you won't hear yourself saying, "I just read two pages and I have no idea what they were about!"

When you read for a main idea, you actively look for the most important thought in the passage. You ask yourself what idea the writer wanted you to know after reading the passage. For example, in the paragraph that follows, what is the main idea? Look for the sentence that tells what the paragraph is about. Is there a clue to the main idea before you even read the first sentence?

> **The Changing Employment Picture**
>
> Today, workers know that what they can expect from employers has changed. Employees used to expect to work for the same company for a very long time. It was not unusual for a person to start working for a company after high school or college and to work there until retirement. Now, young people can expect to change jobs many times during their working years.

Your first clue to the main idea is in the title. After reading the title, you knew the topic of the paragraph. The passage would be about working and about change. Did you know something about this topic? If you did, your mind was jogged to predict what it might be about. You thought it might be about how many people were working. Or, it might be about the different kinds of jobs and where they were available. However, once you read the first sentence, the main idea became clearer. The change you might expect had to do with employers and what workers might expect from them.

> Clue: Topic—The Changing Employment Picture
> Main Idea: Today, workers know that what they can expect from employers has changed.

Now look at the next paragraph in the passage. Remember to keep your mind active as you read: What is the writer's main idea? Where is it placed in the paragraph?

> Job change may occur in the company for which a person has been working; or, job change may mean finding a job in a different company. For example, a person may be hired to do a certain job. A while later, the employer has a different need and asks the worker to do a different job. Or, a person may be hired to do a certain job and, later, the company goes out of business. Either case requires a job change.

Main Idea: Which sentence holds the main idea?

In the preceding paragraph, you found the main idea in the first sentence. If the main idea is not found in the first sentence, where might it be? Sometimes a writer starts a paragraph with a transitional sentence, tying the first sentence to the previous paragraph. You will read more about that later. Or, the writer might want to build evidence in the paragraph. In that case, the writer might start with supporting ideas and work up to the main idea, placing it in the last sentence.

> *Example:* Keep a portfolio of your accomplishments at work and carry that into any meeting about a salary or a raise. If this is a first job, list any internships you may have had during school. These work experiences may add to your salary level. Of course, know what the typical salary level is for a job in your field. If you apply for a job or ask for a raise, certain preparations will help you get a better salary.

Main Idea: Which sentence holds the main idea?

In the preceding paragraph, the writer summarized or added up all the details in the last sentence. That is where you found the main idea. All of the sentences before the last one included a technique for getting a higher salary or a raise.

Other times, the main idea is not stated at all. If that is the case, the reader has to add up the clues and ideas in the reading and reach a conclusion about the main idea. For now, you should know that the main idea is most often found in the first sentence.

Practice 1

As you read each of the following paragraphs, look actively for the main idea. Write the main idea on the line provided.

Paragraph A

Job changes are in your future, so think about how you can prepare. Think about the field in which you want to work. Then look at recent developments. Are there new tools in the field? For example, if you were an administrative assistant or secretary in the past, you will find many changes in that job now. Start with conference calls. Are you familiar with newer tools such as video conferencing or online meeting centers?

Main Idea: *Job changes are in your future, so think about how you can prepare.*

Paragraph B

You can easily discover the occupations that are growing. Go to the website for The Bureau of Labor Statistics for information. You can also find information in your local library. A typical chart will list not only the occupations but also job growth in future years.

Main Idea: *You can easily discover the occupations that are growing.*

Paragraph C

Only twelve years ago, about 25 percent of every dollar spent on food was spent on eating out. Today that amount has doubled. One reason for the change can be traced to both parents, or a single parent, working full time. If you are looking for a career that is growing, keep the food service business in mind.

Main Idea: *First sentence*

Reading for Supporting Details

Try to distinguish between the main idea and supporting details. Start by asking yourself a question: Which sentence is the sum of all the supporting details? That is the main idea. Now you are ready to look at the details.

Go back to paragraph A. How do the other sentences add detail and support to the main idea?

Write the details here:

1._____
2._____
3._____
4._____
5._____
6._____

You probably noticed that each sentence after the main idea adds supporting detail. They tell you how to prepare for job changes in your future. Sentence 2 in the passage asks you to think about the field in which you want to work. Sentence 3 tells you to look at the recent developments you'll need to prepare for that work. Sentence 4 asks you if there are any new tools in the field. Sentence 5 gives a job example, the administrative assistant. Sentence 6 introduces conference call advances. Sentence 7 lists some of the more modern conferencing options.

Practice 2

As you read each paragraph, look first for the main idea. Then list the details that support the main idea.

Everybody's Favorite Food

Paragraph A
You probably know many reasons why people buy over three billion pizzas a year. People of all ages love it. The number of ways pizza can be made is almost endless; it seems to please all tastes and needs. Not only can it be delivered to your door, but it also serves more people for less money.

Main Idea: _You probably know_____

Supporting Details:

1. _____

2. _____

3. _____

Paragraph B
No one will deny that pizza is an extremely popular food, but many would say it is not very good for you. Pizza does contain each of the four food groups. There is grain in the crust, your vegetable—tomato—in the sauce, cheese which is your dairy, and protein in the choice of toppings. It sounds healthful, until you look at the numbers.

Main Idea: _No one will deny_____

Supporting Details:

1. _____

2. _____

3. _____

Paragraph C

One slice of pizza is never enough, so what are you getting in two, three, or four slices? You might think that a plain cheese pizza can't be a problem. That's not true. At a popular pizza chain, three slices of pan crust cheese pizza gives you 12 grams of fat—more than half a day's worth. You also get more than 750 calories and close to a day's worth of sodium.

Main Idea: _____

Supporting Details:

1. _____

2. _____

3. _____

4. _____

Paragraph D

Can you order pizza and not fill your body with fat? Yes, you can. Control the fat by ordering only half the cheese on the whole pizza. With added vegetables and a sprinkle of Parmesan cheese, you won't even miss the fat!

Based on information in "What a Pizza Delivers," from Nutrition Action Health Letter, Volume 29/Number 5

Main Idea: _____

Supporting Details:

1. _____

2. _____

3. _____

Skimming and Scanning

When a question asks you to find a detail, decide specifically what you'll be looking for, and scan all the material for that word or number or phrase. Run your eyes down the middle of the reading, looking only for the item in question. You are not reading for meaning; you are reading to find a specific number, word, or phrase. When you reach the detail, read the words around it to be absolutely sure you have the right one.

Practice 3

Read the following *Employment Trends by Occupation* chart. The topic or main idea of this chart is that trends in employment occur by occupation and over a period of years.

Skim and scan to find the answers to the questions that follow.

Employment Trends by Occupation

Arizona

Occupation	Employment in 2002	Employment in 2012	Percent Change	Job Openings*
Dental assistants	5,280	8,980	+70%	520
Dietetic technicians	890	1,320	+49%	60
Emergency medical Technicians and paramedics	1,540	3,220	+109%	190
All other health practitioners and technical workers	1,390	2,300	+65%	120
Healthcare support workers, all others	2,500	4,230	+69%	220

North Carolina

Occupation	Employment in 2004	Employment in 2014	Percent Change	Job Openings*
Dental assistants	5,890	9,010	+53%	480
Dental hygienists	4,810	7,400	+54%	300
Dietetic technicians	810	1,040	+29%	30
Emergency medical technicians and paramedics	6,360	7,910	+24%	230
Technical workers	3,280	4,260	+30%	160
Healthcare support workers, all other	4,520	5,740	+27%	210

United States

Occupation	Employment in 2004	Employment in 2014	Percent Change	Job Openings*
Dental assistants	267,400	381,700	+43%	18,910
Dietetic technicians	25,200	30,000	+19%	810
Emergency medical technicians and paramedics	191,500	243,700	+27%	7,420
Healthcare technologists and technicians, all other	85,000	104,500	+23%	3,480
Healthcare support workers, all other	202,200	244,500		

*Job Openings refers to the average annual job openings due to growth and net replacement.

Note: The data for the State Trends and the National Trends are not directly comparable. The projections period for the State Trends is 2002–2012, while the projections period for the National Trends is 2004–2014.

1. For which states are you given information in the chart?

   A North Dakota and South Dakota

   B Arizona and New Mexico

   C North Carolina and the United States

   D Arizona and North Carolina

2. How many healthcare support workers were there in Arizona in 2002?

   A 202,200

   B 2,500

   C +69%

   D 2,300

3. True or False? You can directly compare state trends with national trends.

4. In the United States, the largest growth in numbers of jobs was projected in the field of

   A Emergency medical technicians

   B Dietetic technicians

   C Dental hygienists

   D Dental assistants

Practice 4

Read the following introduction and chart. Answer the questions that follow. Use your skimming and scanning skills to find the answers to the questions.

Counting Calories

Each pound of fat your body stores represents 3,500 calories of unused energy. In order to lose one pound, you would have to create a calorie deficit of 3,500 calories. To do that you need to either take in 3,500 fewer calories than you need over a period of time or do 3,500 calories worth of exercise. Experts say that you should not lose more than two pounds (7,000 calories) each week if you want to keep the weight off.

Adding 15 minutes of moderate exercise, for example, walking one mile, to your daily schedule will use up 100 extra calories per day. (Your body uses approximately 100 calories of energy to walk one mile, depending on your body weight.) Maintaining this schedule would use up an extra 700 calories per week, or a loss of about 10 pounds in one year.

Adapted from The President's Council on Physical Fitness and Sports, 2006.

One way to lose weight is to burn more calories by taking more exercise. Following are just a few of the many activities you can use to lose weight.

Calorie and Weight Loss Chart

Exercise	Time Spent	Calories Burned	Results in One Year
Aerobics	10 min./day	83	30,295 cal./8.9 lbs.
Biking	10 min./day	80	29,200 cal./8.3 lbs.
Treadmill	10 min./day	130	47,450 cal./13.6 lbs.
Weightlifting	10 min./day	40	14,600 cal./4.2 lbs.
Bowling	10 min./day	50	18,250 cal./5.2 lbs.

A treadmill is a very effective way to burn calories and therefore reduce body weight. About 10 minutes on a treadmill burns about 130 calories. In one year, this daily fitness workout uses up a total of 47,450 calories—about 13.6 pounds of body fat.

A daily jog on a treadmill doesn't just help you to reduce weight. Like most aerobic exercise, it also helps to lower your risk of developing heart disease and diabetes and improves blood glucose control.

Weightlifting also burns calories and reduces body fat. About 10 minutes of weightlifting burns about 40 calories. In one year, this daily exercise workout uses up a total of 14,600 calories per year—about 4.2 pounds of body weight.

A daily weightlifting workout does more than just help you to build muscle mass. It also helps you to reduce body fat percentage and increases the rate at which you burn calories so you lose weight faster.

1. By skimming the chart, you know that its main idea is
   A A diet plan for the day, week, and year
   B How exercise uses calories and leads to weight loss
   C The difference between protein and carbohydrates
   D The way in which you choose your favorite exercise

2. When you bike, you use
   A 29,200 calories in 10 days
   B 83 calories in a year
   C 8.3 pounds of weight in 10 minutes
   D 80 calories in 10 minutes

3. The two forms of exercise that use the most calories in 10 minutes are
   A Basketball and aerobics
   B Biking and weight lifting
   C Treadmill and aerobics
   D Weightlifting and bowling

Answer Key: Section 2, Lesson 2

Practice 1

A. Job changes are in your future, so think about how you can prepare.

B. You can easily discover the occupations that are growing.

C. If you are looking for a career that is growing, keep the food service business in mind.

Practice 2

EVERYBODY'S FAVORITE FOOD

A. Main Idea: You probably know many reasons why people buy over three billion pizzas a year.

DETAILS:

1 People of all ages love it.

2 The number of ways pizza can be made is almost endless; it seems to please all tastes and needs.

3 Not only can it be delivered to your door, but also it serves more people for less money.

B. Main Idea: No one will deny that pizza is an extremely popular food, but many would say it is not very good for you.

DETAILS:

1 Pizza does contain each of the four food groups.

2 There is grain in the crust, your vegetable—tomato—in the sauce, cheese which is your dairy, and protein in the choice of toppings.

3 It sounds healthful until you look at the numbers.

C. Main Idea: One slice of pizza is never enough, so what are you getting in 2, 3, or 4 slices?

DETAILS:

1 You might think that a plain cheese pizza can't be a problem.

2 That's not true.

3 At a popular pizza chain, three slices of pan crust pizza gives you 12 grams of fat—more than half a day's worth.

4 You also get 750+ calories and close to a day's worth of sodium.

D. Main Idea: You can order pizza and not fill your body with fat.

DETAILS:

1 Can you order pizza and not fill your body with fat?

2 Yes, you can.

3 Control the fat by ordering only half the cheese on the whole pizza.

4 With added vegetables and a sprinkle of Parmesan cheese, you won't even miss the fat!

Practice 3

EMPLOYMENT TRENDS BY OCCUPATION

1. D

2. B

3. False

4. D

Practice 4

COUNTING CALORIES

1. B

2. D

3. C

Most ideas in a passage are directly stated. Other ideas are only suggested. That is why you need to think about what it means to "read between the lines." Obviously, there is nothing written between the lines, but there is an inference, or an *unwritten meaning* for the reader to construct. You will also draw your own conclusions as you read. They are not stated on the page, but become part of your reading experience. By reading between the lines, you will find definitions of new words or clues to their meanings. The last part of this lesson, literary techniques, helps you recognize some of the ways authors use language, style, and technique.

Reading for Inferences

When you read to find an inference, you "read between the lines," figuring out an unstated idea. You are trying to figure out what the writer meant, but did not say. How do you do this?

1. Use the information in the reading.
2. Add your own knowledge to what you have just read.

When you take these two steps, you are reading between the lines, *reading for inferences.* Look at the introductory paragraph before the calorie and weight loss chart on page 32. Answer this question:

If people walk a mile a day and add an extra 100 calories to their diet every day,

A. They will lose at least 10 pounds in 1 year.
B. They will get tired of walking and stop exercising.
C. They will be able to eat an entire pizza and still lose weight.
D. They will not lose 10 pounds because they have added more calories than walking uses up.

Answer: _____

Did you choose D as the correct answer? If you did, you chose the right one. Remember that you are looking for an inference. It's not directly stated but should make sense based upon the facts and your experience. The stem of the question talks about adding an extra 100 calories to the diet daily. Answer A is incorrect because the introduction says that you have to take in fewer calories to lose weight. Answer B is incorrect. As the reader, you have no way of knowing who, if anyone, will get tired of walking. Answer C is also incorrect. From your experience and reading, you know that eating an entire pizza puts weight on people. Answer D is the correct statement. You read that exercise uses calories. However, you know that you have to control the number of calories you take in. The number of calories used up in exercise must be more than the number taken in.

One of the notable things about reading for inferences is that they can be found in almost any kind of reading material. There are even ways to use the skill in reading charts and graphs. Look at the introduction to the weight loss chart on page 32. Answer this question:

Based on the Calorie and Weight Loss Chart, infer the answer to this question: If someone you know dislikes exercising indoors, but wants to lose the most amount of weight in a year, which form of exercise would this person choose?

A Biking

B Aerobics class

C Weight lifting

D Treadmill

You probably chose answer A, biking, as the exercise of choice. The chart doesn't separate indoor from outdoor exercise. From your experience, though, you know that biking is the only one in the list that would most likely be done outdoors.

Practice 1

As you read each paragraph, try to draw inferences from what you read. Answer the questions that follow.

Paragraph A

Whether you have worked for years or are just starting out, you know that getting along with people is an essential skill. The people you work with may be very different from you. Each person has a different personality. Some are easy to get along with; others take special handling. Some people say very little. Others say whatever comes to their minds. They don't mean to upset you, but sometimes they do. Instead of getting angry, take some time to know your co-workers—to study their personalities. Soon you will begin to understand why they talk and act as they do.

Main Idea: _____

Supporting Details:

_____

_____

_____

_____

_____

_____

1. You can infer from this paragraph that people in a workplace
    A Are identical to each other in age
    B Face none of the challenges of getting along with different types of people
    C Need to choose the right time and place to discuss differences
    D Should probably not discuss major differences with people the first day on the job

At work, think of yourself as part of a team and act accordingly. Be ready to contribute ideas and suggestions. Your team members will appreciate your interest in getting things done. When other people on the team do good work, tell them you like what they did. If a team member is sick, offer to help to get the work done on time.

2. From what the paragraph says about being a team player, you can infer that the following is true:
    A You can never interrupt a team at work to suggest a new way to do something.
    B People work better on a team if they know that their work is appreciated.
    C You should never volunteer for extra work under any circumstances.
    D Getting things done is never the important thing for a team.

Paragraph B
As a team member, you have one solution to a problem and your coworker has another. You think the other person just doesn't understand. The fact is that the other person just sees it differently. There is a phrase for that: a difference in *perception*. This is when you need to ask for more information and talk out the possible solutions. If you communicate and try to understand each other, the team will be more productive.

3. Although it is unstated, the main idea of this paragraph is the following:
    A All people on a team perceive things in the same way.
    B Team members never forget to ask for more information.
    C Problems at work often happen when people don't see a situation in the same way.
    D Team members can never be productive.

Paragraph C
Jodi Gast, a top performer for DK Graphics (DKG) of Washington, DC, says she and her manager took a risk on each other seven years ago when she first interviewed with no sales experience. She credits her success with the company to her boss's flexibility.

"I spent my 20's learning about what was important for me in a job, making lots of poor choices, and gaining a lot of wisdom from those choices. I realized that the most important thing for me in a job was having a boss I could respect and like who would respect and like me. I found that at DKG.

After working there for six years, I said 'I'm moving to Florida and I'd like to keep my job.' He immediately said he would work with me to make that happen. The only thing I couldn't do from my new location was input purchase orders. So, we decided to each chip in a small percentage from my sales for the office manager to take on the extra work to assist me.

The only time we had a real problem was in negotiating my maternity leave arrangements. I said, 'I don't think we're coming up with a good creative solution,' so I suggested calling a mediator and, in the process of talking to her, we came up with a compromise that worked out perfectly."

4. It was a risk for Jodi to take the job at DKG because

   A She had no sales experience.

   B She wasn't sure she trusted her boss.

   C She had made a lot of poor choices before.

   D She was moving to Florida.

5. Jodi and her boss used a mediator

   A Because they didn't get along

   B Because she doesn't respect him

   C Because he is inflexible

   D To help them find creative solutions

6. Jodi's boss put extra effort into helping her because

   A She was bringing in more money than his other salespeople.

   B She was highly motivated.

   C They had a good working relationship.

   D All of the above.

Paragraph D

Generations at Work

Four generations now share the workplace. They are often referred to as: The Silent Generation, Baby Boomers, Generation X and Generation Next. In brief, the Silent Generation remembers when the executives were men (in dark suits and white shirts) and the secretaries (in dresses and high heels) used old-fashioned typewriters, carbon paper, and microfiche. Baby Boomers raised the status of women in the workplace and changed traditional notions of family roles at home. Gen Xers grew up alongside the technology boom. They brought a wave of dress-down, flextime, work-at-home, and play-at-work attitudes to the office. Gen Nexters come to the table with technology as a second skin. The first rung on the corporate ladder is not always their first step. Their workplace is so different from the one where the Silent Generation got its start, that a Nexter might guess that microfiche is a small French fish. However, specific age groups and profiles of each group are less important than understanding some common issues that arise when generations come together at work.

Adapted from Perfect Phrases for Motivating & Rewarding Employees, by Harriet Diamond and Linda Eve Diamond, McGraw-Hill, 2006.

7. You can infer from the article that the oldest generation mentioned is

   A Generation Next

   B Generation X

   C The Silent Generation

   D Baby Boomers

8. You can infer from the article that the youngest generation mentioned is

   A Generation Next

   B Generation X

   C The Silent Generation

   D Baby Boomers

9. Which generation does the author say "raised the status of women in the workplace"?

   A The Silent Generation

   B Generation Next

   C Generation X

   D Baby Boomers

10. What does the author mean by the statement, "Gen Nexters come to the table with technology as a second skin"?

    A Generation Next was born knowing computers.

    B Generation Next was raised using computer technology from an early age.

    C Generation Next is the smartest of the four generations.

    D No one from other generations can possibly learn all that a "Gen Nexter" knows about computers.

11. From the passage, you can infer that microfiche is

    A An old system for storing information

    B An old style of clothing

    C A dance

    D A small French fish

Practice 2

Study the following protein content charts. Then read the passage. Use the information from the form and the passage (using your knowledge of main ideas, supporting details, and inferences) to answer questions 1–6.

Protein in Raw Nuts and Seeds (shelled)

Nut/Seed (1/4 cup)	Protein Grams
Almond	7
Cashew	4
Peanut	8
Pecan	2
Pumpkin Seed	7
Sesame Seed	7
Sunflower Seed	8
Walnut	5

Protein in Beans (cooked)

Bean (1 cup)	Protein Grams
Black Beans	15
Black-eyed Peas	14
Cannellini (White Beans)	17
Fava Beans	13
Kidney Beans	15
Lentils	18
Lima Beans	15
Soybeans	29
Split Peas	16

Protein in Fresh Vegetables (cooked)

Vegetable	Serving Size	Protein Grams
Artichoke	medium	4
Asparagus	5 spears	2
Beans, String	1 cup	2
Beets	1/2 cup	1
Broccoli	1/2 cup	2
Brussels Sprouts	1/2 cup	2
Peas	1/2 cup	4
Peppers, bell	1/2 cup	1
Potato, baked with skin	2 1/3 × 4 3/4"	5
Potato, boiled with skin	1/2 cup	1
Squash, Summer	1 cup	2
Squash, Winter	1 cup	2
Sweet Potato	1 cup	3

Protein in Soy Products

Product	Serving Size	Protein Grams
Tofu		
Medium to Extra Firm	3 oz.	7 to 12
Tofu		
Soft or Silken	3 oz.	4 to 6
Textured Vegetable Protein		
TVP	1/4 cup	10 to 12

Isabelle is a nurse who has been advising patients that vegetarian diets do not have enough vital proteins. She has recently been told by her new supervisor that a good vegetarian diet is rich with protein. He gave her a booklet with the preceding tables, which use figures from the USDA Nutrient Database. People are often surprised to learn that all plant foods contain at least some protein.

1. The tables are used to show that
   A Vegetarians need more protein.
   B People can get enough protein without eating meat.
   C Protein can only be found in meat or fish.
   D Fish and meat are higher in protein than vegetables.

2. According to the chart, 1/4 cup of sunflower seeds has
   A 2 grams of protein
   B 6 grams of protein
   C 8 grams of protein
   D No protein

3. According to the chart, extra firm tofu has
   A More protein than soft tofu
   B Less protein than soft tofu
   C The same amount of protein as soft tofu
   D Half the protein that soft tofu has

4. The charts do not show the protein content of
   A Meat, chicken, and beans
   B Meat, potatoes, and peas
   C Fish, chicken, and meat
   D Fish, pork, and beans

5. According to the passage,

   A All plants contain protein.

   B Only plants that grow upright contain protein.

   C Only plants that grow on a vine contain protein.

   (**D**) Not all plant foods contain protein.

6. Which of the following statements is Isabelle likely to say to a patient?

   A Everyone should be a vegetarian.

   (**B**) You should eat meat for protein, but eat some vegetables.

   C Broccoli is the best source of protein.

   D Good vegetarian diets have ample amounts of protein.

Reading to Draw Conclusions

You just learned about reading for inferences. Reading for inferences and drawing conclusions are closely connected. Inferences are *unstated*. Drawing conclusions involves making judgments or decisions based on the facts *stated in the reading*. You add your experience, or the facts you already know, to draw conclusions. What conclusion can you draw from the following passage?

> Anyone who takes medications should observe certain precautions. For example, check to see if your name is on the prescription label and that it is, in fact, the correct medication. Then check the expiration date. A medication that is past that date may not do what it was prescribed to do. Always dispose of medications carefully. In addition, the medications should be stored under the right conditions, in a cool, dry place. Finally, always take medications at the right time and in the right amount.

The passage states that old medications should be disposed of carefully. This is done so that

A. The house stays neat and clean.

B. No money is wasted.

C. No one will find and take the wrong medicine.

D. People will always have to buy new medications.

Did you choose Answer C? If you did, you were right. Everything in the paragraph is about precautions that need to be taken. You can conclude that the only way you can be absolutely sure the medicine won't be taken by mistake is to dispose it of carefully.

Practice 3

As you read the following passages, try to draw a logical conclusion from what has been stated.

Passage A

The employees reported that 80% of their bad moods at work were caused by conflicts. Their anger and frustration from the conflicts led to less work getting done. It made sense for them to fix the conflict. They knew that would make them feel better and they would get more done.

The group worked with a team expert to develop a list of ideas to make unhappy relationships better. Her first suggestion was to emphasize the positive: Look for the good in people. This doesn't mean you have to like the people. You just have to recognize the good things about them—their skills and strengths—and concentrate on those.

The employees learned that change doesn't result from just the other person changing. The team expert asked everyone in the group to look at themselves. Each person was to ask what he or she could change about him or herself.

Finally, the group learned to attack the problem, not a person. They brought their team together to identify the problems first.

1. The group probably chose to work with a team expert because
   A Without help from an expert, they knew they could never get anything done.
   B Each person knew it was impossible to change anything.
   C The company was going out of business, and everyone needed to be educated.
   D Without help, their history of conflict wouldn't allow them to fix the problem.

Passage B

Why do companies use advertising to sell their products? The answer, of course, is that the product almost never sells itself. Instead, the sale is made when the ad ties the product to something else that's important to the reader. For example, people value beauty, success, and love. What happens when we see a glass of milk in the hands of a beautiful woman or a handsome man? Another ad shows a car driven by a young, well-dressed person. These images sell products.

2. According to the passage, which of the following is true?
   A We are convinced by certain images to buy products.
   B A sale is never made as a result of an advertisement.
   C People will buy anything that is advertised.
   D Only very young people buy advertised products.

Passage C

When you buy a book or a CD, you pay the store. At a football game, you pay to attend. Then, you buy a souvenir from a vendor. If you're hungry, during the game, you buy food at the counter or from a vendor who's walking through the crowd. But, if you're watching the game on TV, how do you pay for it? The answer is that you pay for it indirectly by buying the advertisers' products.

3. You can conclude that

A There is no cost to the TV station when it shows a football game.

B Only the hotdog vendors pay for the game to be on TV.

C Advertisers buy time on TV to showcase their products.

D There is no benefit to advertisers from showcasing their products on TV.

Understanding Words in Context

We don't always know the exact meaning of all the words that we read (or hear). Of course, it is not practical to carry a dictionary all the time. However, good readers (and listeners) use certain techniques to figure out what is being said. You can use a helpful procedure to figure out the meaning of a word. That is, you examine the *context,* or situation, in which it is used. You check for clues in the words and sentences that surround the unknown word. Checking the main idea and tone of the whole article will also provide clues to word meanings.

STUDY TIP 1
Look at the word or words *immediately following* the word that you don't understand. Are commas or parentheses setting off those words? If so, the words within those punctuation marks may explain what the unknown word means. If not, look for clues in the sentences *just before or after* the word.

Example: Reread the paragraph preceding the study tip. Find the word *context.* Now look at the words *or situation* that follow. What do you think? If you are thinking that *situation* is another way to say *context,* you are correct. These two words are synonyms, words that mean more or less the same thing. Writers will often place synonyms immediately before or after difficult words. Notice that the word *synonym* is defined, or explained, in the sixth sentence of this paragraph.

Complete these sentences:

1. Synonyms are _____.

2. Another word for *defined* is _____.

You should have completed Sentence 1 with *words that mean more or less the same thing.* The answer for Sentence 2 is *explained.*

STUDY TIP 2
Look for patterns in the sentences that surround the unknown word. Do you see a group of words repeated two or more times? Are they also next to or near the unknown word? Writers sometimes structure the way they say things in order to help the reader get the message. They may purposely repeat groups of words in a sentence or paragraph for emphasis.

Example: Look back at the first paragraph of ": Understanding Words in Context" on page 44. Locate and underline the group of words that is repeated in the third and fourth sentences.

Did you underline the phrase *figure out* twice? Now circle the words that come before each of those phrases. Notice that these words—*technique* and *procedure*—have a similar meaning: they are both *a system,* or *a way,* to accomplish something—in this case, *a system to figure out the meaning* of words.

STUDY TIP 3

Many words have more than one meaning. Sometimes you need to see a word used in a specific situation to know what it means. Often, the topic or the main idea of the passage will help you to interpret the meaning of individual words.

Example:

1. I was *down* for three days in bed with the flu. A friend unknowingly gave me the *virus* when she sneezed.
2. My computer system was *down* for three days after my friend unknowingly sent me an e-mail that was infected by a *virus.*

In both sentences, the word *down* means, "not working as usual." However, in Sentence 1, "down" means "in poor health." In Sentence 2, it refers to "in mechanical failure." Likewise, the word *virus* has two different meanings in the context of these sentences. In both cases, *virus* refers to something that has caused trouble. The system has stopped functioning normally. However, in the first sentence, *virus* means a biological organism that causes an illness. In the second sentence, *virus* means a piece of programming code that can cause damage to computer files.

CONTEXT CLUE: ANTONYMS

The opposite of *synonym* is *antonym.* Antonyms are opposites of words. For example, some antonyms are *believe* and *disbelieve, opposite* and the *same,* and *calm* and *excited.*

In the following sentences, choose an antonym that completes each sentence:

1. Because we have so many of the (same/opposite) values, we get along very well.
2. I prefer (old/new) movies because I love great special effects.
3. The new hospital library is the result of (stingy/generous) donations.

The only choices that logically complete the sentences are (1) same, (2) new, and (3) generous.

Practice 4

Identify the meaning of the words in *italics* in the following sentences: (Hint: Use Study Tip 1.)

1. In response to the stress of tiring exercise, the human body produces chemicals called *endorphins,* the body's natural pain relievers.

   Endorphins are

   A A reaction to emotional stress

   B Safe medication for humans

   C Painkillers produced by the body

   D Chemicals known as dorphins

2. The professor wrote my user name and password on the top of my copy of the course *syllabus,* which outlines topics she will cover in her class.

   A syllabus is

   A A list of books

   B A password to study materials

   C Related to the syllables of words

   D An outline of what will be studied

In the sentences that follow, look for the similar word patterns that help define the words in *italics.* (Hint: Use Study Tip 2.)

3. Teaching about morphemes is an effective way to improve students' reading comprehension. Teaching about word parts that have meaning— prefixes, suffixes, and roots—helps students improve their understanding of what they read.

   Morphemes are

   A Vocabulary definitions

   B Parts of words that have meaning

   C Form of an organism

   D Related to a student's reading speed

4. It took Andrew eight years to complete the coursework he needed before he could start the Registered Nursing Program. Then he discovered there was another kind of *prerequisite* he needed before he started—basic computer skills.

   Prerequisite means

   A A skill

   B A requirement for nurses

   C An exam

   D Something required ahead of time

5. *Consumption* of *legumes* in the United States is quite low. The average *per capita consumption* is about one pound per person each year. That means the average person eats just over one ounce of beans a month.

From the context of these sentences, you can figure out that:

(Write your answers.)

A *Legumes* are _____.

B *Consumption* means _____.

C *Per capita* means _____.

Choose the meaning of the selected words in the context of these sentences. (Hint: Use Study Tip 3.)

6. The *mouse* rolled across the smooth top of the computer desk and fell with a crash on the tile floor. *Mouse* means

    A A small rodent with a long tail

    B A small stuffed animal

    C A small facial bruise, usually around the eyes

    D A small device used to make selections on a computer screen

7. The suspect's testimony provided the detective with the missing *link* he needed to solve the crime. *Link* means

    A An association of detectives

    B One of the connecting parts of a metal chain

    C Word or icon connecting web sites

    D Information needed to uncover other information

Read the following selection. Pay special attention to the words in *italics*. Answer the questions that follow.

The World Wide Web (www.) is a system that uses the Internet to link information to the world. The Web offers many different resources. Libraries, newspapers, shopping malls, telephone directories, and more exist on a *global* scale. As it continues to change and expand, the Web is becoming an enormous *repository* of human culture. The Web is a storage area for information about different ways of life.

Why has the Web become so popular? For the most part, it is a user-friendly information access tool. Also, it is fast and as easy to use as the nearest online computer. No wonder it is quickly becoming the research tool of choice. Experienced Web users can *readily* obtain information while saving time and energy. Indeed, young people today seem to know *intuitively* how to use the Web, without having to ask. Learning opportunities are available to users of all ages, providing unlimited education at a distance. It is true that there are many irritatingly commercial, money-seeking sites. But there are many other sites that are wonderfully *altruistic*. Many sites offer information, services, and products for free.

Use the context clues in the preceding paragraphs to select the meaning of these words:

8. Altruistic

   A Wonderful

   B Generous

   C Have an attitude

   D True to their word

9. Global

   A On a small scale

   B Shaped

   C Worldwide

   D Lighted

10. Repository

   A A place for safekeeping

   B A large container

   C A deposit box

   D A main storage area

11. Readily

   A Gathering

   B Easily

   C Prepared

   D Steady flow

12. Intuitively

   A Naturally

   B Bravely

   C Conclusively

   D Invitingly

Reading to Recognize Literary Techniques

Certain reading skills are associated with essays, autobiographies, and fiction. You need to recognize the special use of language, plus the author's purpose, style, and technique.

In the early 1800s, the American author Washington Irving wrote a story called *The Legend of Sleepy Hollow*. That story is still well-known today. Read a passage from the story and answer the questions that follow.

On the eastern shore of the Hudson River lies a small market town or rural port known as Tarry Town. This name was given by the good housewives from the propensity of their husbands to linger about the village tavern on market day. Not far from this village there is a little valley among the high hills which is one of the quietest places in the whole world. A small brook glides through it with just murmur enough to lull one to repose. This sequestered glen has long been known as Sleepy Hollow by Washington Irving.

Adapted from The Legend of Sleepy Hollow by Washington Irving

The author used vocabulary that

  A Suggests great activity

  B Tells you how very noisy it was

  C Describes all the animals in the area

  D Describes a quiet, sleepy village

Answer _____

Did you choose D as the correct answer? If you did, you were right. Answer A is incorrect because the passage does not mention activity at all. Answer B is incorrect also. In fact, the paragraph has a number of words that have to do with being quiet. Answer C is incorrect since no animals are mentioned. Answer D is correct. How does the author's vocabulary, or choice of words, tell you that this is a quiet, sleepy village? Look at Sentences 3, 4, and 5. The author uses the words *quietest places, murmur enough to lull one to repose,* and *Sleepy Hollow.* The vocabulary certainly sets a quiet scene.

Now think about the author's purpose for writing this particular passage. You could assume that the author's purpose for writing this passage was to

  A Express very strongly what he disliked about the area

  B Set the scene, or describe, the place in which the story would be set

  C Show how very much he disliked all the characters in his story

  D Give a detailed descriptions of the houses in the village

Answer A is incorrect since the author likes the area. Answer C is incorrect. The paragraph has almost no information about characters in the story. Answer D is also incorrect since the houses are not described. Answer B is correct: the paragraph is included to describe the place.

Now read more of *The Legend of Sleepy Hollow,* and answer the questions that follow. As you read, think about why the author went to such lengths to introduce the "spirit."

Some say the place was bewitched by a German doctor in the early days of the settlement. Others say that an old Indian chief, the wizard of his tribe, placed a spell over the good people. The townspeople are all given to marvelous beliefs and subject to spells and trances and visions and frequently see strange sights.

The dominant spirit, however, that haunts this enchanted region, and seems to be commander-in-chief of all the powers of the air, is the apparition of a figure on horseback without a head.

The author used the opening paragraph to

    A Give the story a happy-go-lucky feeling and a happy ending

    B Explain how much the townspeople disliked each other

    C Describe an Indian tribe

    D Convince the reader that these people would believe in a headless horseman

What was the author's purpose for the first paragraph? If you chose answer D, you were correct. The first paragraph talks about spells, beliefs, trances, visions, and frequently seen strange sights. These were people who could be convinced to "see" a headless horseman.

Practice 5

Read the passages. Read to discover the author's point of view, style, and purpose. Notice how language is used. The Practice begins with another passage from *The Legend of Sleepy Hollow,* by Washington Irving. Try to visualize the main character as you read.

> In this place of nature, there abode a man by the name of Ichabod Crane who sojourned, or as he expressed it, "tarried," in Sleepy Hollow. He was there to instruct the children of the vicinity. The name of Crane was not inapplicable to his person. He was tall, but exceedingly lanky, with narrow shoulders, long arms and legs, hands that dangled a mile out of his sleeves and feet that might have served for shovels, and his whole frame most loosely hung together. His head was small, and flat at top, with huge ears, large green glassy eyes, and a long snipe nose so that it looked like a weather-cock, perched upon his spindle neck, to tell which way the wind blew. To see him striding along the profile of a hill on a windy day, with his clothes bagging and fluttering around him, one might have mistaken him for the spirit of famine descending upon the earth, or some scarecrow eloped from a cornfield.
>
> His schoolhouse was a low building of one large room constructed of logs . . . The schoolhouse stood in a lonely but pleasant situation just at the foot of a woody hill . . . A brook ran by and a large birch tree grew at one end of it. From there the low murmur of his pupils' voices, conning over their lessons might be heard on a drowsy summer's day, like the hum of a bee-hive. Interrupting now and then was the voice of the master, in the tone of menace or command. Sometimes one heard the appalling sound of the birch, as he urged some tardy loiterer along the path of knowledge. Truth to say, he was a conscientious man, and ever kept in mind the golden maxim, "Spare the rod and spoil the child." Ichabod Crane's scholars certainly were not spoiled.
>
> *Adapted from* The Legend of Sleepy Hollow

1. The author uses descriptive language to give you a picture of Ichabod Crane. Which set of the following words is most descriptive of Ichabod?

    A Conscientious, thin, menacing, narrow shouldered

    B Spared the rod and spoiled the children

    C Hum of a bee-hive, sound of the birch

    D Low building, one large room, at the bottom of a hill

2. The words "the low murmur of his pupils' voices" and "the appalling sound of the birch" are used for descriptive

    A Nonsense

    B Contrast

    C Menace

    D Lessons

3. The phrase, "the spirit of famine" strongly suggests that Ichabod

    A Never ate a meal in his house or anyone else's

    B Was an enormous scarecrow in the field

    C Appeared to be the picture of a starving person

    D Overate at breakfast, lunch, and dinner

Answer Key: Section 2, Lesson 3

Practice 1

Main Idea: Whether you have worked for years or are just starting out, you know that getting along with people is an essential skill.

DETAILS:

- The people you work with may be very different from you.
- Each person has a different personality.
- Some are easy to get along with; others take special handling.
- Some people say very little.
- Others say whatever comes to their minds.
- They don't mean to upset you but sometimes they do.
- Instead of getting angry, take some time to know your co-workers—to study their personalities.
- Soon you will begin to understand why they talk and act as they do.

1. D
2. B
3. C
4. A

5. D
6. D
7. C
8. A
9. D
10. B
11. A

Practice 2

PROTEIN CONTENT CHART

1. B
2. C
3. A
4. C
5. A
6. D

Practice 3

1. D
2. A
3. C

Practice 4

1. C
2. D
3. B
4. D
5. beans, eating, per person
6. D
7. D
8. B
9. C
10. D
11. B
12. A

Practice 5

1. A
2. B
3. C

Reading Skills Posttest

Read the passage and answer questions 1–3.

People use e-mail because it is so convenient and fast. Writers like the informality of e-mail. The question is, can informality be carried too far? If you are writing to a friend or family member, informality is acceptable. If you are writing an e-mail at work, think again. Even if you are on friendly terms with your boss, you need to think about the impression your e-mail makes. Any spelling or grammar mistakes you make may be seen by many people!

In an e-mail to a friend, you might not use a salutation (Dear Amy, Dear Ron). Instead you might start your message, the text, immediately.

From: Ken Lester KenL@abcinc.com
To: Ron Mott ronm@coolco.com
Subject: Lunch
Date: January 12, 2008

I'm leaving for lunch at 1. Where do you want to go?

How does the above e-mail differ from the business e-mail that follows?

From: Ken Lester KenL@abcinc.com
To: Ron Mott ronmott@coolco.com
Subject: Luncheon meeting
Date: January 12, 2008

Dear Mr. Mott,

I am looking forward to our luncheon meeting today. I hope that 1 PM is still good for you. If so, I will see you at The Greenhouse Café at 1 PM.

1. A main feature of e-mail is its

   A   Friendship and informality

   B   Impression and friendliness

   C   Formal salutation and speed

   D   Speed and convenience

2. A conclusion you can draw about writing an e-mail is that

   A   No one really likes receiving an informal e-mail.

   B   Your word choice depends upon how well you know the recipient.

   C   A salutation is never necessary.

   D   E-mail is never appropriate in business.

3. The author cautions e-mail writers

   A   Not to write to the boss

   B   To skip the subject line

   C   To check spelling and grammar

   D   Not to include a salutation

Read the chart and answer questions 4–8.

National Statistics

	2004	2003	2002	2001	2000	1999	1998	1997	1996	1995	1994
Motor Vehicle Traffic Crashes											
Fatal Crashes	38,253	38,477	38,491	37,862	37,526	37,140	37,107	37,324	37,494	37,241	36,254
Traffic Crash Victims											
Occupants											
Drivers	26,756	26,779	26,659	25,869	25,567	25,257	24,743	24,667	24,534	24,390	23,691
Passengers	10,304	10,458	10,604	10,469	10,695	10,521	10,530	10,944	11,058	10,782	10,518
Unknown	82	104	112	102	86	97	109	114	103	119	109
Nonmotorist											
Pedestrians	4,641	4,774	4,851	4,901	4,763	4,939	5,228	5,321	5,449	5,584	5,489
Pedalcyclists	725	629	665	732	693	754	760	814	765	833	802
Other/Unknown	128	140	114	123	141	149	131	153	154	109	107
Total	42,636	42,884	43,005	42,196	41,945	41,717	41,501	42,013	*42,065	41,817	40,716
Other National Statistics											
Vehicle Miles Traveled (Billions)	2,923	2,890	2,856	2,797	2,747	2,691	2,632	2,562	2,486	2,423	2,358
Resident Population (Thousands)	293,655	290,789	287,941	285,102	282,192	272,691	270,248	267,784	265,229	262,803	260,327
Registered Vehicles (Thousands)	237,961	230,633	225,685	221,230	217,028	212,685	208,076	203,568	201,631	197,065	192,497
Licensed Drivers (Thousands)	198,889	196,166	194,602	191,276	190,625	187,170	184,861	182,709	179,539	176,628	175,403
National Rates: Fatalities											
Fatalities per 100 Million Vehicle Miles Traveled	1.44	1.48	1.51	1.51	1.53	1.55	1.58	1.64	1.69	1.73	1.73
Fatalities per 100,000 Population	14.52	14.75	14.94	14.80	14.86	15.30	15.36	15.69	15.86	15.91	15.64
Fatalities per 100,000 Registered Vehicles	17.92	18.59	19.06	19.07	19.33	19.61	19.95	20.64	20.86	21.22	21.15
Fatalities per 100,000 Licensed Drivers	21.44	21.86	22.1	22.06	22.00	22.29	22.45	22.99	23.43	23.68	23.21

* Total fatalities for 1996 include two fatalities of unknown person type.

from the National Center for Statistics and Analysis (NCSA) http://www-fars.nhtsa.dot.gov/main.cfm

Think about the skimming and scanning skills you learned as you answer these questions:

4. According to the chart, fatal crashes have

   A   Increased since 1994

   B   Increased every year since 1994

   C   Doubled since 1994

   D   Decreased since 1994

5. Accidents involving pedestrians

   A   Increased since 1994

   B   Increased every year since 1994

   C   Doubled since 1994

   D   Decreased since 1994

6. Miles driven have

   A   Increased since 1994

   B   Increased every year since 1994

   C   Doubled since 1994

   D   Decreased since 1994

7. Miles traveled are measured in the

   A   Thousands

   B   Millions

   C   Billions

   D   Trillions

8. According to the chart, how many people were victims of traffic accidents in 1998?

   A   37,107

   B   24,743

   C   131

   D   41,501

Read the passage and answer questions 9–14.

Getting Organized

Your physical environment plays a significant role on your mental state. Clutter in the home and workplace often adversely affects clear thinking and productivity. However, most of us have become junk collectors. We're compelled to buy stuff we don't want, don't need, and may never even use.

We get frustrated because we can't find important items we really need amidst the junk. Do you have junk-filled drawers or closets? Can you even see the surface of your desk? Freeing yourself of the excess will not only clear your space and allow you to make important items easier to find and keep handy, it will help clear your mind and create a more relaxing atmosphere.

If you have a hard time deciding what to keep and what to toss out, consider these clutter-clearing guidelines:

Clothing—If you haven't worn it in the last year, let it go. If you didn't feel the need to wear that old purple striped sweater in the last 365 days, are you really going to wear it in the next 365?

Tools and Kitchen Utensils—If you have more than two of the same thing, get rid of the extras. How many hammers or coffee mugs do you really need? Are they ever all used at once?

Food—Is your kitchen cluttered with food you never touch or don't get to until it's green and fuzzy? Sure, make an exception for a great sale and stock foods that keep well, but avoid excess foods that will lead to overeating and spoilage.

Start small with a cluttered pantry, desk, or single closet. Once you start clearing out, you'll feel so good that the momentum just might carry you to the next cluttered space and then the next. In time, you can transform your living and work spaces.

So what do you do with all that stuff? Take your excess and have a garage sale, sell it online, or donate it. Someone else can use what's junk to you and when you clear it out, you'll find you not only have more space, but more peace of mind.

9. "Clutter in the home and workplace often adversely affects clear thinking and productivity." *Adversely* means

   A Positively

   B Negatively

   C Blindly

   D Awkwardly

10. "We get frustrated because we can't find important items we really need amidst the junk." *Amidst* means

    A Outside of

    B Among

    C Inside

    D Over

11. The author says buying excess food leads to

    A Overeating and clutter

    B Clutter and mess

    C Spoilage and overeating

    D None of the above.

12. "Once you start clearing out, you'll feel so good that the momentum just might carry you to the next cluttered space and then the next." *Momentum* refers to

    A The energy of forward movement making you want to keep going

    B The exhaustion from cleaning all day

    C A momentary break from activity

    D Slowing down

13. The author says you should take items you no longer use and

    A Sell them or give them away.

    B Break them.

    C Wrap them and give them as holiday gifts.

    D All of the above.

14. The author's tone is

    A Formal and firm

    B Casual and friendly

    C Sad

    D Angry

Read this article and answer questions 15–19.

EarthSave Member Spotlight

Mary Ann Lederer, EarthSave Cincinnati Member

EarthSaver Mary Ann Lederer feels lucky. Never mind that she's been in a wheelchair 24 years, ever since an intruder shot her in the spine. Never mind that she has "absolutely horrid health problems" and almost died twice.

Lucky?

"Everywhere I go, everything I do, I find something exciting and good," she says.

Right now, Ms. Lederer is too busy to go looking for *anything*. She's in a frenzy preparing for yet another show of her paintings. This one, opening July 8 at Mullane's Gallery, coincides with her 60th birthday.

Sitting in the living room of her tiny apartment surrounded by her paintings, she promises to be there: "The thing is, I have to lie down a lot, so I don't go out much anymore. I spent years trying to get people used to the wheelchair and seeing me carried up steps. But now, because of a cyst on my spine, I have to lie down to deal with the pain. So I'll have a couch at Mullane's. You think people will ever get used to seeing someone lying on a couch in a restaurant?"

"I want a kind world," she says. "We too often look for bad guys to blame when we should be giving hugs. Police brutality, racism, the death penalty, they all have to go and be replaced with hugs."

Ms. Lederer practices what she preaches. She's a vegetarian of long standing and an avid organic gardener who relies on friends to help out. She donates paintings to any group with a cause she likes. She's a member of several human rights organizations, and though she can't man the picket line, she still helps. Recently, she painted 40 picket signs for a protest march.

She's also serious about making the world a better place, and for her, that begins with kids: Every Christmas, she collects upwards of 700 books for the neighbor kids in her low-income apartment complex—"because they should read," she says. "They *need* to read, but they don't always have the opportunity. Our complex, usually you only hear about it when there's a police run. I hire the kids, too. Small jobs, like taking out the garbage or running to the store or picking up garbage from my garden. Sometimes, just to reach something on a top shelf. And they love it. Don't let anyone tell you kids don't want to work."

"The reason I don't go out alone anymore is because I'm too brittle. Not long ago, I was alone getting out of my car and into my chair. I fell and wedged myself between the chair and the car. If the kids hadn't come along and lifted me into my chair, I'd have been there a long time." She says it again: "I was lucky. See what I mean?"

Somehow you do.

Source Info: "Painting a gentler world" by Zim Knippenberg. It appeared in The Cincinnati Enquirer on June 24, 2001.

15. Mary Ann Lederer's role in the EarthSave organization is as a

A   Member

B   President

C   Artist

D   Painter

16. She lies on a couch during her art exhibit because

A   She gets tired.

B   She gets bored.

C   She has a cyst on her spine.

D   She can.

17. She tries to make the world a better place by

A   Collecting and donating books for children

B   Donating her paintings

C   Painting picket signs

D   All of the above.

18. She believes that kids

A   Don't want to work

B   Want to be helpful

C   Read too much

D   Are lazy

19. The author is impressed that Mary Ann feels lucky because

A   She has such a wonderful attitude.

B   Children are a great help to her.

C   She is a vegetarian.

D   She is in a wheelchair with terrible health problems because of being shot in the spine.

Read the passage and answer questions 20–24.

Peaceful Money Management for Couples

by Kathy Miller

Regardless of how much or how little people have, money is the most common cause of dissension in relationships. While each couple is unique, most arguments about financial matters start with either lack of organization or lack of communication. Following are some tips for peaceful money management:

Get organized. Create systems that work for both people. Choose one place for checkbooks, receipts, and other information regarding financial transactions. Use a file marked "Payables" for credit card statements, monthly mortgage, car, and insurance payment booklets, utility bills, etc., which should all be kept together until they have been paid.

Put details in writing. Many people carry their financial information around with them in their heads—the monthly direct debit for the health club membership, the month they renew their auto insurance, the day they promised to pitch in for Aunt Martha's new sofa bed. While the ability to remember facts and figures is impressive, all that information takes up prime real estate in your mind. Did you know Albert Einstein could not recite his telephone number from memory? He saved the space for new ideas. Getting all those details out of your head and onto paper will help you feel more peaceful while making the data more accessible to your partner.

Schedule a "money meeting." Sit down with your partner regularly to discuss your finances. Arrange all information about what bills are due, how much is due, and the date each payment is due into an easy-to-read format. Together, go over your expenses, compare your monthly income to your monthly expenses, and brainstorm solutions to problems that arise or ways to increase income. For instance, if you find your paycheck will not cover the new computer equipment your son needs, you could choose to take action on selling that timeshare in Orlando or the treadmill-turned-coat-hanger that is collecting dust in your basement. Maybe you have medical bills you have been meaning to submit to the insurance company for reimbursement. You might decide it is a good idea to take on a part-time job or pick up an extra shift at work. The point is to think of solutions together.

The money meeting is meant to empower you. While facing the facts and figures may be disheartening or upsetting at first, remind yourselves that sometimes the problem gets bigger before it gets better. In order to prevent the session from turning into an argument, preface your meeting with an agreement about what you will do when tensions rise. Some couples choose to light candles and take deep breaths; others take a walk or drink a cold glass of water. You could consider having an objective third-party sit with you the first few times.

If you find yourselves in trouble, get help right away. Do not make a bad situation worse by delaying action. Professional counseling and coaching services are available, and sometimes one session is all it takes to get you back on track. Learn how to make money a positive force rather than a destructive force in your relationship. If there are real problems, they will be easier to face when you face them together.

www.agoodsteward.net

20. The main idea of this article is

    A Couples should work together to manage their money.

    B Couples should be in business together to make money.

    C Couples always fight over money management.

    D Money management is stressful and should not be discussed.

21. "Money is the most common cause of dissension in relationships." *Dissension* means

    A Agreement

    B Agreeing to disagree

    C Disagreeing about the relationship

    D Disagreement

22. According to the passage, the most important reason to write down payment due dates is

    A   Because even Einstein didn't remember everything

    B   So that your partner knows them, too

    C   So you don't forget

    D   So your partner will think you're organized

23. The money meeting is meant to empower you. *Empower* means

    A   To find power through money management

    B   To take power away from

    C   To give power to

    D   To want to help

24. The point of a money meeting is to

    A   Get your partner to stop spending

    B   Find financial solutions together

    C   Make money

    D   Apologize for overspending

Looks Too Good To Be True

Every day, American consumers receive offers that just sound too good to be true. In the past, these offers came through the mail or by telephone. Now the con artists and swindlers have found a new avenue to pitch their frauds—the Internet. The on line scams know no national borders or boundaries; they respect no investigative jurisdictions. But, as with all scammers, they have one objective— to separate you from your money!

An interesting point about fraud is that it is a crime in which you decide whether or not to participate. Hanging up the phone or not responding to shady mailings or e-mails makes it difficult for the scammer to commit fraud. But con artists are very persuasive, using all types of excuses, explanations, and offers to lead you—and your money—away from common sense.

Education, good judgment, and a healthy dose of skepticism are the best defenses against becoming a victim. Remember, if it looks too good to be true, it probably is!

Adapted from LooksTooGoodToBeTrue.com

25. Which of the following statements best sums up the author's warning?

A Everyone will be swindled at one time or another.

B If an offer sounds too good to be true, be careful!

C Never give your credit card over the Internet.

D The Internet should not be used for money transfers.

26. Which of the following is not stated as a way to protect against fraud?

A Education

B Good judgment

C Not responding to shady e-mails

D Buying computer spam filters

27. The purpose of this piece is to

A Warn people to be careful

B Point out how gullible people are

C Let scammers know how easy it is to fool people

D Get people to buy a product

28. The article says fraud is a crime in which you decide to participate, meaning

A You have no legal course of action.

B You can often protect yourself by using good judgment.

C If it happens to you, it is obviously your own fault.

D You are just as responsible as the swindlers.

Read the following passage and answer questions 29–32.

Listening Experience

by Linda Eve Diamond, author and ListenersUnite.com Site Author

I have 38 years of intermittent listening experience. I was in the corporate training field, writing and teaching about communication skills for nearly fifteen of them. I also spent ten years on a listening intensive project known as marriage. Prior to that, I was a teenager with an outstanding capacity for listening when I felt like it and when I wasn't otherwise distracted. I was also having the acute but common experience of feeling that *no one* listened.

I had gained some experience on that front as a child. I doubted more and more whether people listened or could really understand each other, but I talked to them anyway—just in case. Much of my childhood was spent discovering that life was not lived within one righteous, objective truth. One of the great hurdles of my young days was accepting that when things got hopelessly tangled, no superhero was going to swoop down and untangle them, illuminating us all to the great objective truth.

In the beginning, I made some noise, but mostly I listened. Earlier memories are a little hazy and muffled, but I know I lived by my mother's heartbeat and life hasn't had quite such a steady rhythm since then. I think I sometimes miss those days. Or the time prior still (when *anything* was possible), when there was no need of rhythm at all or language, hormones, or perspectives. But here I am. And life has its own boundless advantages.

One of the great advantages of life is the capacity to connect with others and true connection comes from listening. Like everyone, I have my own listening strengths and challenges, but I enjoy the deeper levels of connection that come from careful listening. I've even started to listen more diligently to myself, which led me to follow my heart and create ListenersUnite.com.

www.ListenersUnite.com

29. In the first paragraph, the author injects a tone of

- **A** Terror
- **B** Disinterest
- **C** Humor
- **D** Hysteria

30. You can conclude that the author considers listening

- **A** Just another skill you have to learn when you retire
- **B** Necessary only if you are married
- **C** Necessary if you want to get a good deal on a car
- **D** Necessary if you want to connect with others

31. In the third paragraph, the author says, "Earlier . . . I know I lived by my mother's heartbeat . . ." You can infer from this that

    A   She's talking about the time before she was born.

    B   She is talking about her relationship with her mother.

    C   She loves her mother.

    D   None of the above.

32. What is one of the main ideas the author offers about listening ability?

    A   Only teenagers have it.

    B   Everyone has strengths and challenges.

    C   We only hear noise.

    D   No one listens to children.

Read these safety instructions and answer questions 33–37.

Workplace Safety

This section from a company manual gives employees instructions on how to avoid a painful workplace injury called carpal tunnel syndrome.

Carpal tunnel syndrome, a nerve disorder in the hand, can be caused by the repetitive movements of typing on the computer. The syndrome is a form of RSI, repetitive strain injury. If you feel pain, numbness, or tingling in your wrists or hands, please notify your supervisor and go to a doctor immediately. Other early signs are shooting pains from the wrist up the arm or a burning feeling in the fingers. Early treatment can help prevent serious harm.

We provide ergonomic keyboards, designed for comfort and safety. There are also things you can do to avoid the problem. Adjust computer screens and keyboards to reduce strain. Your keyboard should be elbow level so that your forearms, wrists, and hands are in line with, or parallel to, the floor. Please use the wrist pads provided by every keyboard and mouse. We also urge you to review and use the enclosed exercises that reduce strain and the risk of carpal tunnel syndrome.

If you choose to wear a wrist brace, please shop for one on our doctor-approved list or one that your own doctor recommends. Some of the braces sold inhibit muscle use more than necessary, which is also not good for muscle health. The recommended braces are proven safe and effective. If you have any questions, please call Human Resources.

33. Carpal tunnel syndrome is

   A A nerve disorder

   B A contagious disease

   C A workplace solution

   D A sudden accident

34. *RSI* stands for

   A Repetitive syndrome incidents

   B Repetitive strain injury

   C Redundancy syndrome instance

   D Reactivated syndrome increase

35. *Ergonomic* means

   A Dangerous

   B A nice looking design

   C Designed for comfort and safety

   D Having to do with money

36. If your forearms are parallel to the floor, they are

   A In line with the floor

   B Pointing down toward the floor

   C On an angle to the floor

   D Touching the floor

37. In "some braces inhibit muscle use," *inhibit* means

   A Practice

   B Encourage

   C Overextend

   D Hold back

Read the following play and answer questions 38–42.

The Wave

by Michael Diamond

Harold and Mary, a married couple who appear to be in their sixties, have just exited a lawyer's office and are walking through a small park that is dotted with shade trees and benches. He has just signed a living will, a document that names someone responsible for making a life or death decision for you if you, because of accident or illness, are unable to make a decision. Of course, that's a possibility no one wants to think about.

HAROLD: You know, you're supposed to feel better after you sign one of those things.

MARY: The living will?

HAROLD: The living will. (He pauses.) I don't feel better.

MARY: Forget about it. We go on with our lives. Believe me, in a week or two you won't even remember what you signed or what you said in that office.

HAROLD: I'll remember. I said not to bother too much keeping me alive. If it looks like I'm cooked . . .

MARY: Cooked? That's funny. (Mary laughs and kisses Harold on the cheek. She holds his arm as they walk.)

HAROLD: . . . then, pull the plug. Rip out the tubes. Nothing to eat or drink. In a couple of days, I'm on my way to a refrigerator with a tag on my big toe that says Harold Macy was here. But he's not here any more.

MARY: Harold, that's awful. Why are you making such a big deal now?

HAROLD: Because I never really thought about it before. If I'm not here—and that's what it's going to say on my big toe—then, where *am* I?

MARY: Harold, you're sixty-seven years old. Don't tell me you never thought about death before. I heard you say it, many times, that you'll meet your father and your brother, Eddie, when you die. Oh, yeah and you'll meet your first wife, too. But you weren't going to talk to her up there. And you always said that you looked forward to pulling up a cloud and sitting down for a long talk with your father, the kind of talk he didn't have time for when he was alive. You said all that, didn't you?

HAROLD: (Pauses to think.) I said it.

MARY: Your pop will be glad to see you. You'll tell him that the Red Sox won the World Series. He'll say, "Why did I have to die so soon?" And then you'll tell him which of those men hit home runs and . . .

HAROLD: Quit it, Mary. I never meant any of that. I never imagined an end. It was all talk— talk to take up time.

(Harold sits on a bench. Mary sits next to him.)

HAROLD: You know how we sometimes say that we're doing things to take up the time? You know, so that life doesn't drag on too much? We do the crossword puzzle. You talk to your sister. We take a walk, and all of a sudden, it's time for lunch. And that was how we took the time up. Well, that's what my talking about death was about. A little noise to fill the time. And it made me feel smart. But I never imagined . . .

MARY: So, now that you see an actual ending to the life of Harold A. Macy, where do you think what's left of him might go after the refrigerator door closes on his torso that's covered by a sheet?

HAROLD: Mary, all I can see him doing is looking at the top of the inside of a refrigerator. It's a stainless-steel drawer. And he's saying get me the hell out of here.

MARY: Okay. So death is the end. There is nothing else. Done. Gone. Harold used to be, and then he wasn't any more.

HAROLD: That's why you put down for them to use every means? No tubes are too many. "Keep me alive for as long as there are trees." That's exactly what you said. The lawyer laughed. He asked you to add that sentence, at the end of the will in your own handwriting.

MARY: Well, I know there's nothing else. Once the door is closed on life, that's it. Candle out. Done. And we're all yesterday's sushi that gets thrown out with the trash.

HAROLD: But what if there's more? Really. What if there's more? And what if the people on the other side know all about us?

MARY: Cut it out, Harold. You don't understand what you're talking about.

HAROLD Wait a minute . . . A wave. Did you feel it? I just felt it. Eddie and pop must have moved, like in a pool, and I felt the ripple. Mary.

MARY: Harold, this is ridiculous. That was me standing up. What you felt was . . .

HAROLD: Please. Something happened. I don't know what to say or how to say it. Something . . . (long pause) . . . like what we live for.

MARY: Children feel things that go bump in the night.

HAROLD: Yes. And if they say something that doesn't sound real, we tell them they're wrong. We tell them they imagined their bumps in the night.

MARY: I never heard you talk like this.

HAROLD: And I never . . .(Looks into the distance. Begins to talk. Says nothing.)

MARY: Harold.

HAROLD: I made the right choice. There's nothing to be afraid about. Only . . .

MARY: Only?

HAROLD: They'll ask us what we've done.

MARY: You mean? . . .

HAROLD: Not if we rooted for the Red Sox. I don't think I'll ever use those words again: "filling up the time."

MARY: Harold, when we get older, we sometimes begin to get a little strange. Those around us are supposed to tolerate us, even through we're strange. That's what I'm doing now. Watch the game. I'll make corned beef, the way you like it.

HAROLD: I don't think so. Maybe some other night.

(They walk off the stage together.)

Excerpted from *The* Wave, by Michael Diamond

38. The tone of the language in this play is

   A   Conversational

   B   Formal

   C   Grammatically unacceptable

   D   Too casual to be true

39. Mary and Harold's relationship is

   A   Loving

   B   Warlike

   C   Honest

   D   Answers A and C

40. You can infer that Harold

   A   Has not had any conversations with Mary before this time

   B   Will ask his lawyer to cancel the living will

   C   Has just begun to think seriously about the end of his life

   D   Believes he has an illness and will die soon

41. Some years ago, Harold

   A   Was 67 years old

   B   Was divorced

   C   Decided not to marry again

   D   Left Mary for another woman

42. The title, *The Wave,* refers to

   A   Harold's feeling that he sensed the presence of his father and brother

   B   Mary feeling a wave of anger that Harold wasted their time if he didn't want a living will

   C   The feeling of moving through life, as if through a pool

   D   Harold thinking about waving goodbye to life

Read this article on resume writing. Then answer questions 43–44.

The Last Step

If you have applied for a job, you've probably written a resume. Through the resume, an employer learns about your job history, your schooling, and your qualifications. But the resume doesn't do the entire job. It doesn't match your background to the specific job in an employment ad. That can only be done by a strong cover letter.

Some people wonder why they have to have a super-star cover letter if they have a well-written resume. There are several good reasons. First, employers receive many, many resumes and they often don't read them carefully. You want to get the reader's attention with a well-written cover letter that highlights your particular qualifications. In the letter, you can highlight the specific skills and experience that do apply to the job at hand.

What do you need to include in a cover letter? Actually, there are only two elements but they are extremely important. First, the cover letter should highlight your qualifications for the job. Second, the letter should point to the parts of the resume that relate your qualifications to the specific job. The reader must see this connection if you expect to be given an interview.

You can include the important elements above in a four-paragraph cover letter. Remember to include the following:

1. Why you are the person for the job

2. Your successes at your current job

3. How your skills and experience connect to the job you're seeking

43. The main idea of this passage is that

    A Employers read all resumes thoroughly.

    B A brief cover letter is always OK.

    C A cover letter only has to state your interest in the job.

    D A strong cover letter is as important as a well-written resume.

44. You can infer from this passage that a cover letter and resume

    A Are unnecessary when you apply for a job

    B Are very important because they introduce you to the employer

    C Don't need to be perfect in spelling and grammar

    D Will never "sell" you to an employer

Answer Key: Section 2, Lesson 3 (Posttest)

1. D	**2.** B	**3.** C	**4.** A	**5.** D	**6.** B
7. C	**8.** D	**9.** B	**10.** B	**11.** C	**12.** A
13. A	**14.** B	**15.** A	**16.** C	**17.** D	**18.** B
19. D	**20.** A	**21.** D	**22.** B	**23.** C	**24.** B
25. B	**26.** D	**27.** A	**28.** B	**29.** C	**30.** D
31. A	**32.** B	**33.** A	**34.** B	**35.** C	**36.** A
37. D	**38.** A	**39.** D	**40.** C	**41.** B	**42.** A
43. D	**44.** B				

To ensure that you have mastered the skills in the Reading Section:

1. Once you have checked your answers against the answer key, go back to compare your incorrect answers with the correct ones. Notice whether you understand why the answer given is the correct one.

2. Total your number of correct answers out of the 44 possible answers. If you had **fewer than 40 correct answers**, find the sections that explain your incorrect answers and review them carefully. If you had **fewer than 38 correct answers**, take some extra time to go back through the reading section. Look at each incorrect answer throughout the chapter and go back to the corresponding lesson to see that you understand why each answer given is the correct one.

3. Before taking the TABE test, come back to review the Reading Section. Pay special attention to areas that were difficult or confusing, but scan the entire chapter again to make sure that you feel confident in knowing and using these skills.

SECTION 3 | Language

LESSON 1 Getting Started

Following is a shortened version of the Lesson 1 language questions in the original TABE Level A book. If you filled out this section in the original book, think about whether your goals have changed. You may want to fill it out again. If you did not fill it out before, take some time to complete this section.

Reflection: Writing in My Daily Life

I estimate that I write _____ hours a week (including personal emails or letters and work-related tasks).

I want to improve my ability to write _____ for my personal satisfaction.

I want to improve my ability to write _____ for job or career advancement.

Composition

I am able to organize my thoughts and express myself clearly when I write.

_____ Yes _____ No _____ Need practice _____ Don't know

Editing

I am able to correct my own writing.

_____ Yes _____ No _____ Need practice _____ Don't know

I know how to check it for:

Plan, purpose, and tone	_____ Yes	_____ No	_____ Need practice	_____ Don't know
Correct use of words	_____ Yes	_____ No	_____ Need practice	_____ Don't know
Complete sentences	_____ Yes	_____ No	_____ Need practice	_____ Don't know
Organized paragraphs	_____ Yes	_____ No	_____ Need practice	_____ Don't know

Spelling	____ Yes	____ No	____ Need practice	____ Don't know
Punctuation	____ Yes	____ No	____ Need practice	____ Don't know
Capitalization	____ Yes	____ No	____ Need practice	____ Don't know

Spelling

I am able to identify the correct spelling of a word when I am given more than one choice.

             ____ Yes ____ No ____ Need practice ____ Don't know

I can identify the correct spelling of a word by the way it looks.

                                         ____ Yes ____ No

I can identify the correct spelling of a word by knowing the rules.

                      ____ Yes ____ No ____ Need to review the rules

Language Skills Pretest

Read the following e-mail. Use it to answer questions 1–3.

Subject: The New Insurance Plan

Our new health care plan has a number of wellness incentives, so please review your new insurance packet carefully. A points program allows each employee to pay less depending upon involvement in wellness activities. For instance regular attendance at a health club or our series of upcoming nutrition seminars will save you money on your insurance plan. Nonsmokers gain points as do those who use any one of a number of stop smoking methods.

---

1. Choose the phrase that should be followed by a comma:

    A Our new health care plan,

    B A points program,

    C For instance, ✗

    D upcoming nutrition seminars,

2. A comma should be inserted following the words:

    A attendance at a health club,

    B will save you money,

    C Nonsmokers gain points,

    D who use any one of,

3. An apostrophe is correctly used in which of the following:

    A incentives'

    B series'

    C point's program

    D None of the above

Read these paragraphs from a company manual. Each is a segment taken from a longer discussion. For questions 4–14, look at the numbered underlined parts, and choose a word or phrase that best fills those spaces.

Company Manual

Website's "Employees Only" Area

(4) The company <u>are taking</u> a new approach to the sign-in procedure. Please signed in using your employee ID number. The first time you sign in, (5) <u>you will have asked to enter</u> a password. (6) <u>Passwords is private</u> and should not be shared with anyone. This site will keep you informed of company news and events. (7) <u>All employees had signed in</u> every morning to find company news and updates.

4.

A   The company won't be taking

B   The company is taking

C   The company some time in the future are taking

D   The company lost some time but are taking

5.

A   you will be asked to enter

B   you will be asked to have entered

C   you will be asked to be entering

D   you will ask to enter

6.

A   Passwords, is private

B   Passwords: are private

C   Passwords are private

D   None of the above

7.

A   All employees should signing in

B   All employees, should sign up

C   All employees should be signed

D   All employees should sign in

Coworker Feedback

Website's "Employees Only" Area

(8) Many employees want to know what the procedure is for giving peer <u>evaluations?</u> We encourage informal feedback among coworkers. However, we discourage any negative remarks (9) <u>such as You didn't do a good job.</u> Your feedback should always (10) <u>be helpful specific and timely.</u> Say how you were affected, not what your coworker did wrong. (11) You can tell a coworker <u>that you missed your morning break because of the rush caused when he or she came in late</u>.

8.

   A   evaluations.

   B   evaluations!

   C   , evaluations.

   D   Evaluations:

9.

   A   such as "you didn't do a good job."

   B   such as, "You didn't do a good job".

   C   such as, "You didn't do a good job."

   D   Correct as is

10.

   A   helpful specific, and timely.

   B   helpful; specific; and timely.

   C   helpful: specific; and timely.

   D   helpful, specific and timely.

11.

   A   that, "You missed your morning break because of the rush caused when he or she came in late."

   B   that, "You missed your morning break because of the rush caused when he or she came in late".

   C   that: You missed your morning break because of the rush caused when he or she came in late.

   D   Correct as is

(12) <u>And positive feedback</u>. (13) Everyone can use some praise for a <u>job done good</u>. Even the (14) <u>President</u> of the company can use a pat on the back.

12.

    A   And positive feedback?

    B   Positive feedback.

    C   Positive feedback is important.

    D   Positive feedback is important?

13.

    A   job done better.

    B   job done best.

    C   job well done.

    D   Correct as is

14.

    A   president

    B   "President"

    C   President:

    D   Correct as is

For questions 15–17, read the paragraphs from a resume. In each case, choose the sentence that best fills the blank in the paragraph.

15. _____.

I have always had an interest in photography and have recently started selling photographs to my local newspaper. My real interest is in portrait photography.

    A   I am writing in for the job.

    B   I hear you need a new assistant?

    C   In response to your Daily News ad, I am coming in for an interview.

    D   I am writing in response to your Daily News ad for a photographer's assistant.

16. I have been to your portrait studio and am always impressed with the unique, natural poses. _____.
I can assist in any way you need, including taking photographs, setting up shots, lighting, processing, and working with customers.

    A   I love to work with animals, especially.

    B   I love to work with people and am eager to learn and to support your work.

    C   I think I can show you a thing or two, also.

    D   I didn't like the photograph of the two little girls; the composition was all wrong.

17. _____.

A small portfolio is included with my resume to show my techniques and perspective.

    A   I am experienced in restaurant management, too.

    B   I am experienced in Photoshop Elements and have been shooting with a Canon 20D.

    C   My mother says I have an eye for photography and I take great pictures of my kids.

    D   Look, enclosed, at the pictures I took with my new Canon 20D.

Read the following sentences. For questions 18–24, choose the sentence that is written correctly *and* shows the correct capitalization and punctuation.

18.

    A   The President, the Managers, and the staff all agree.

    B   For once, President Macy agrees with the board.

    C   The board is in agreement they met this morning.

    D   The speaker, Eddie Howell, of Crocker Industrials.

19.

    A   I gave the report to my boss that was complete.

    B   Janice and me are going to the library.

    C   Bernice and I was working together last summer.

    D   Olivia and I joined a book club together.

20.

    A   The meeting will begin promptly at 8:00 A.M.

    B   Jim and Peter, housemates for 11 years can't agree on anything.

    C   Lets go shopping tomorrow afternoon.

    D   Iris left for Europe this morning; she will be gone for three weeks.

21.

    A   We lived on the south side of westfield township.

    B   The article titled: "Why Care"? was about how environmental issues affect us.

    C   Dora asked, "why don't you ever come in on time"?

    D   Jim sneered and said, "I'll come in when I want to."

22.

   A Howard and Rita are a young, athletic couple.

   B George is always efficient, punctual, and thinks in a creative way.

   C The company gave Nabil an expenses account to take clients out to fancy Restaurants.

   D He uses his expense account for food, clothing, and to travel.

23.

   A The exercise class was difficult, because I'm so out of shape.

   B This morning, the instructor asks us if we want to try the next level.

   C I would like to teach a yoga class and incorporate hints on handling daily stress; someday I will.

   D I would like to teach a yoga class and one day I will.

24.

   A I need more office supplies, including highlighters, legal paper, and index cards.

   B The office store, is on your way home, would you mind picking up these supplies?

   C My accountant told me to save receipts however I hardly ever remember.

   D I have been out of work for four months; because a good job is hard to find.

For questions 25–27, choose the answer that best completes the sentence.

25. All of the employees _____ going out on strike.

   A are

   B is

   C are gone

   D are striking

26. My job seems _____ than yours.

   A more easier

   B most easier

   C easier

   D easiest

27. My last job _____ much more challenging.

   A was

   B is

   C has been

   D were

In questions 28–30, read the underlined sentences. Then choose the answer that best combines those sentences into one.

28. <u>We closed the store.</u>

<u>The big chains were coming into town and we couldn't compete.</u>

  A We closed the store and as a result the big chains were coming into town and we couldn't compete.

  B We closed the store and the big chains were coming in and we couldn't compete.

  C We closed the store when the big chains were coming in and couldn't compete.

  D We closed the store because the big chains were coming in and we couldn't compete.

29. <u>My boss and I have become good friends.</u>

<u>We have discovered, through working together, that she and I have a lot in common.</u>

  A My boss and I have become good friends through working.

  B My boss and I realized that we have a lot in common and have become good friends.

  C My boss and I have a lot in common like good friends who work together.

  D My boss is my best friend.

30. <u>My resume is strong.</u>

<u>But what people notice most is that I worked for Spike Lee for two weeks.</u>

  A Although my resume is strong, what people notice most is that I worked for Spike Lee for two weeks.

  B Although my resume is strong, I worked for Spike Lee for two weeks.

  C Because I worked for Spike Lee for two weeks what people notice is mostly it.

  D My resume is strong because I worked for Spike Lee for two weeks.

For questions 31–32, read the paragraph. Then choose the sentence that does *not* belong in the paragraph.

31. (1) A new furniture store is having a grand opening sale on Sunday. (2) I need new furniture and may go to see what they have. (3) I recently redecorated my kitchen, replacing the sink and all the old appliances.

A Sentence 1

B Sentence 2

C Sentence 3

D Correct as is

32. (1) I don't like the decisions of the new school board. (2) My sister-in-law is on a school board. (3) I am going to educate parents about their latest decisions, which I feel are not good for our children. (4) If all of the parents stand together against the board, we can make a difference.

A Sentence 1

B Sentence 2

C Sentence 3

D Sentence 4

For questions 33–34, choose the word or phrase that best completes the sentence.

33. The old office was so _____; I like our new modern look.

A older

B more older

C old fashioned

D older fashion

34. Katherine didn't _____ to bring her notes to the meeting.

A remember

B remembers

C is remembering

D have remembered

Answer Key: Section 3, Lesson 1 (Pretest)

1. C	**2.** C	**3.** D	**4.** B	**5.** A
6. C	**7.** D	**8.** A	**9.** C	**10.** D
11. D	**12.** C	**13.** C	**14.** A	**15.** D
16. B	**17.** B	**18.** B	**19.** D	**20.** D
21. D	**22.** A	**23.** C	**24.** A	**25.** A
26. C	**27.** A	**28.** D	**29.** B	**30.** A
31. C	**32.** B	**33.** C	**34.** A	

To discover your areas for skill improvement in the Language Section:

1. Once you have checked your answers against the answer key, go back to compare your incorrect answers with the correct ones. Notice whether you understand why the answer given is the correct one.

2. Total your number of correct answers out of the 34 possible answers. If you had fewer than **31 correct answers,** pay special attention to this chapter and be sure to take the Language Posttest.

3. After completing the chapter, go back to review the Language Pretest questions that you answered incorrectly to see if you have a better understanding of why the answer was incorrect.

Look at your results on the language pretest. Find the areas you need to strengthen. Although we suggest that you review and practice all language areas covered in this section, pay special attention to the items that you found difficult.

If you have forgotten—or never really learned—the names, definitions, and uses of grammatical terms, don't worry. Many of the explanations and reminders in this book discuss important concepts and usage without using complex grammatical terms.

Parts of a sentence can be defined in two ways: (1) by using their names and (2) by knowing their job.

1. Each word in a sentence has a *name,* such as: *noun, pronoun, verb, adjective,* etc. Example:

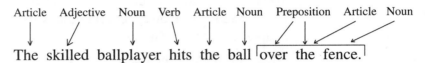

2. Each of those above-named words has a *job* to do in the sentences we construct. For example, nouns either function as performers or receivers (known in grammatical terms as the subject or the object); verbs are *action* or *being* words, pronouns are words that *take the place of other words*; and adjectives *describe other words.*

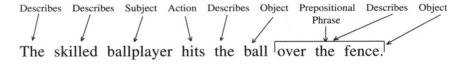

Sentence Types

The four basic sentence types:

*   Statement: You wrote that letter.
*   Question: Did you write that letter?
*   Exclamation: You wrote that letter!
*   Command: Write that letter.

The action word in the sentences above is *write/wrote.* In all four, the performer is *you.* In the fourth sentence, *you* is not written, but it is *implied* in the command.

More commands:

Arrive on time tomorrow!

Hand in your papers.

Turn off the lights before you leave.

Pronouns

A *pronoun* is a word that can take the place of the name of a person, place, or thing (otherwise known as a *noun*).

Example:

Name/Noun

Paulo is a graphic artist.

Or

Pronoun

He is a graphic artist.

The pronoun *he*, in place of *Paulo*, acts as the subject just as the name, *Paulo*, does in the first sentence.

He is a subject pronoun. *Subject* and *object pronouns* are simple grammatical terms that are helpful to remember to avoid some of the most common pronoun errors. If the pronoun is used to represent the subject of a sentence, always use a pronoun from the subject column.

Pronoun Chart

	Subject	Object
1st Person (the person or people speaking)	I, we	me, us
2nd Person (the person or people spoken to)	you	you
3rd Person (the person or people spoken about)	he, she, it, they	them

Example of common pronoun error:

Paulo and me are graphic artists.

Or

Me and Paulo are graphic artists.

"Me" cannot be used as the subject; it is the wrong pronoun for this job. The second sentence commits the same pronoun error and another, putting *Me* before *Paulo*. (Just remember to be polite and not mention yourself first!)

LANGUAGE TIP

When two performers (Paulo and I) undertake the same act or are connected in the same way to the object (*are* graphic artists), you can use a simple trick to avoid an error. Eliminate the name, *Paulo,* and test the sentence. For example: If I eliminated Paulo, would I say or write the sentence this way?

Me am a graphic artist.

No, I would say:

I am a graphic artist.

Therefore: Paulo and *I* are graphic artists.

Practice 1

Pronouns whose job it is to be the subject are *I, you, he, she, it, we, they.*
Choose one of these pronouns to replace the incorrect one in each of these
sentences.

1. Ray and me left the office at the same time.

_____

2. Her and Annie are in the same class.

_____

3. Leslie and him worked on the project together.

_____

4. Me and Val met online in a chat room.

_____

5. Me and Harry are stepbrothers.

_____

6. Quincy, Beth, and me are cousins.

_____

7. Him and Sonya invited Quincy, Beth, and me to the party.

_____

8. Lorna and me are partners.

_____

Personal Pronouns

There are a number of different kinds of pronouns. Here is a list of pronouns that you use very often. They are called *personal pronouns.*

	Singular	Plural
1st Person (the person or people speaking)	I, me, my, mine	we, us, our, ours
2nd Person (the person or people spoken to)	you, your, yours	you, your, yours
3rd Person (the person or people spoken about)	he, him, his she, her, hers it, its	they, them, their, theirs

Keep in mind what you already learned about subject and object pronouns. *Me, us, him, her,* and *them* are *always* object pronouns. Below are
examples of both object and personal pronouns.

Examples:

The books are *yours.* They do not belong to *her.*

What's *mine* is *yours.* Everything here is *ours.*

He planted roses for *me* in *my* garden.

Another Pronoun Problem

Whether a pronoun is singular or plural, it should be consistent throughout the sentence or series of related thoughts.

For example:

A freelancer sets up their own hours.

The sentence above is *incorrect. Freelancer* is the subject and it is singular. *Their* is a plural pronoun that refers to *freelancer.* Either both words must be plural or both must be singular.

Corrections:

A *freelancer* sets up *his* or *her* own hours.

Or

All *freelancers* set up *their* own hours.

Sometimes plural words come between the subject and the referring pronoun:

Each one of the employees has their own website.

Each is still the singular subject. No matter how many plural words follow the subject, the next pronoun must be singular.

Correction:

Each one of the employees has *his/her* own website.

Practice 2

Choose the correct pronoun in each of the sentences below. Two sentences are correct.

1. All new employees must have his or her forms filled out before the first day of work.
2. Ingrid told the supervisor her's e-mail was not working.
3. Each of our children wants a room for themselves.
4. They are reaching the stage where they want to have their privacy.
5. Anybody who thinks they know everything are sadly mistaken.
6. Rebecca and Tom are both working in his and hers family businesses.
7. Herb and Toni are each taking the exam.
8. Bill and Calvin are both contributing to the charity from his paycheck.
9. Lorna and I are saving us money for a trip.
10. Each Isabelle and Carlos are saving for their retirement years.

Subjects and Verbs: Singular and Plural

Performers and actions have to agree in time and number. What does this mean? It means, first of all, that actions agree with performers in number: singular or plural.

Tito arrives at work at 8:00 A.M.

The action word is *arrives*. The performer is *Tito*. What changes take place in the following sentence?

Tito and Jenna arrive at work at 8:00 A.M.

Because the sentence has more than one performer, the action word takes a slightly different form: *arrive* instead of *arrives*.

This may not seem logical to you because an *s* at the end of a word in English often signals more than one, or plural. (For example, the plural of *performer* would be *performers*.) But an *s* at the end of an *action* word means just the opposite. Add an *s* to an action word in order to agree with the *singular* performer, and remove the *s* to agree with the plural performer. Most of the time, we seem to do this correctly without even thinking.

Tito arrives.

Tito and Jenna arrive.

Sometimes an extra word or two in the sentence fools us.
Example:

A new feature of the software make it easier to use.

This sentence is *incorrect*. The sentence talks about the subject, *feature*. The subject is singular. What is the action word or verb? It is *make*. Put those two words together without extra words between them, and how would you write them?

A new feature make it easy to use.

Or

A new feature makes it easy to use.

The second is correct because *feature* is singular and *makes* is singular; they agree.

Practice 3

Read each sentence. Decide whether the subject and verb agree in number. Correct any errors. Only one sentence is correct.

1. This wildlife reserve, untouched by any developers, are home to hundreds of species.

    _____

2. A credit card with any of those banks charge a high interest rate.

    _____

3. The book, *Eats Shoots and Leaves,* are a best seller.

_____

4. The man at the counter need a refill for his fountain pen.

_____

5. Brenda type faster than anyone else in the office.

_____

6. This online store, with hundreds of products, needs to be better organized.

_____

7. The art fair go on rain or shine.

_____

You want to write about more than one person or thing (a compound subject) in a sentence. That makes the subject plural, and the action word/verb follows suit.

Example:

Larry and Maureen go out to breakfast every morning.

The action word/verb in the sentence is *go.* If the subject were *Maureen,* how would the action word (verb) change? Remember what you read above. You add an *s* to the action word (verb) if the subject is singular.

Maureen *goes* out to breakfast every morning.

Note: *Is* and *are* are also verbs—their action is to *link* words. You will read and practice more with these later.

Practice 4

Circle the correct action or linking word (verb).

1. Red and blue (is/are) our school colors.
2. Nathan and his partner (is/are) scheduling the grand opening for next month.
3. Luis and Carole (play/plays) in the company softball league.
4. Donya (write/writes) for a magazine in New York.
5. The new supervised playground (provides/provide) the children with a safe place to play.
6. The student and her parents (is/are) invited to attend the award ceremony.
7. The author, Frank McCourt, and his agent (is/are) speaking at the writer's conference.
8. The singer and his backup band (tour/tours) all over the world.

More Challenges

What other subject-verb agreement challenges do you need to know about? A few word combinations cause many common writing and speaking errors.

- **The subject contains an *either/or* combination:** Think of the subject as *either* one *or* the other, which makes the subject singular. Choose a singular verb.

  Either *Wayne or Joe* plans the event every year.

- **The subject is compound and contains an *either/or* combination:** The verb is singular or plural depending on the number of the second subject word.

  Either *my sister* or *her children* plan the holidays.

  Sister and *children* are the two subject words. *Children* is the second subject word and it is plural; therefore, the plural verb form, *plan*, is correct.

- **The subject of the sentence is *any*:** *Any* is singular and used when the choice involves three or more, but remember the choice leaves *one* (any *one*), which is singular. Choose a singular verb.

  Any of your teachers *takes* that challenge.

  (This is true unless: Any *two team members are* welcome to team up for this project.)

Practice 5

Choose the correct verb in each sentence.

1. Either this photo or that one (work/works) in the advertisement.
2. Any one of those jackets (match/matches) the outfit.
3. Beverly and her brother (go/goes) to the same school.
4. Both this book and the DVD (offer/offers) unique perspectives on history.
5. This set of dishes (make/makes) a great housewarming gift.
6. The children always (laugh/laughs) at the characters in the story.
7. Each child (try/tries) to copy the comical voices of the narrators.
8. The mail and calendar programs (is/are) not working properly.
9. Ray has 300 CDs and (is/are) always buying more.
10. The store (sell/sells) used DVDs for as little as $4.99.

REVIEW

Practice 6

Correct each sentence. Look for errors in subject-verb agreement use of pronouns as subjects, and use of special constructions.

1. Drew and ~~me~~ *I* share an office.
2. Drew and ~~me~~ *I* ~~shares~~ share the workload, too.
3. Vic and I ~~goes~~ *go* to school together.
4. Lorna's car ~~need~~ *needs* a tune-up.
5. Ethan Jesse or Tamara ~~decorate~~ *decorates* the store for Halloween.
6. Robert and ~~me~~ *I* are engaged.
7. We all ~~goes~~ *go* to the gym every morning.
8. Both of us ~~needs~~ *need* to be at the meeting.
9. Derek, the manager, and ~~me~~ *I* are working together.
10. ~~I and Suzanne~~ *Suzanne and I* created the slideshow.

The length of a sentence does not determine whether it is complete; a sentence is only complete if it has the two essential elements: subject and verb. A phrase that does not contain a subject and verb is a fragment, not a sentence. Consider the following examples:

I ran.

Standard office procedure manuals in the human resources office.

The first is a complete sentence, even though it has only two words. The second is a fragment. Where is the verb? A complete sentence would be "Standard office procedure manuals *are* in the human resources office." *Or* "Standard office procedure manuals in the human resources office *are* extras for anyone who needs another copy."

Practice 7

In this practice, look for statements that are not complete thoughts. Rewrite them. Some of the statements are complete thoughts and won't require rewriting.

1. About my resume. *is complete*

_____

2. My resume and application. *are ready to submit*

_____

3. Return the movies. *if you don't want to pay a fine*

_____

4. Information enclosed.

_____

5. When information is enclosed.

_____

6. In schools where languages are taught.

_____

7. Mailed Thursday.

_____

8. When money is tight.

_____

9. Bring it home.

_____

10. On time arrivals and departures.

_____

Practice 8

Read the following paragraph taken from a memo. Find any errors. Rewrite the paragraph to correct those errors.

> About dress down days. We needs to discuss what is appropriate. What guidelines can we set? Dressing down doesn't mean undressing. Us and members of the board are concerned about what clients will think. We don't want to take away dress down days. New guidelines coming.

Verbs and Time

Verbs also indicate time, or what grammarians call tense. For the most part, we use simple tense correctly—drive, drove, will drive—without even thinking about it. More complex tenses change verb forms and use what we call "helping verbs" (or "helping words").

Present	Past	Future	Past plus helping word _has, have, had_
Plan	planned	will plan	has, have, had planned
Walk	walked	will walk	has, have, had, walked
listen	listened	will listen	has, have, had listened
count	counted	will count	has, have, had counted
use	used	will use	has, have, had used

Study the very specific uses of tense to indicate time in the following examples:

Present tense takes place now or is a statement of fact.

Examples:

Victor *plans* our conferences.

We *hold* our conferences in spring.

Present continuous tense is ongoing, happening up to and including the present moment:

Example: Victor *is planning* the conference.

Present continuous tense with helping words *has been* or *have been* is also ongoing, up to and including the present moment.

Example: Victor *has been planning* the conference this year.

Present continuous with helping word *had* happened before another time to which the speaker is referring. (Look for signal words such as *since* and *before*.)

Example: Victor *had been planning* the conference this year before Victoria took over.

Past tense happened in the simple past.

Example: Victor *planned* the first conference.

Past tense verb with helping word *has* or *have* has a number of uses. It can show a past event that continues into the present or an event that occurred at some unknown or unimportant time in the past (often used to talk about experiences and often used, in this instance, with *ever* or *never*).

Examples:

Victor *has planned* our conferences for the last six years.

I have never been to Bermuda.

I have lived here for two years.

Past tense verb with helping word *had* happened in the past, before another time to which the speaker is referring. (Look for signal words such as *since* and *before*.)

Example: Victor *had planned* our conferences before Victoria took over. She *has been planning* them for two years now.

Future is the simple future tense.

Example: Victoria *will plan* our conference from now on.

Additional Examples:

I **drink** two cups of coffee every day.

I **am drinking** two cups of coffee every day.

I **have been drinking** two cups of coffee every day.

I **had been drinking** two cups of coffee every day before I gave up caffeine.

I **drank** two cups of coffee every day last week.

I **have drunk** two cups of morning coffee before.

I **had drunk two cups of coffee** before I remembered the effect too much caffeine has on me!

I **will drink** two cups of coffee tomorrow morning.

Practice 9

Part A
Place these action words on the chart. The first word, *call,* is done for you.

Present	Past	Future	Past plus helping word *have*
call	called	will call	have called
want			
walk			
vote			
use			
type			

Part B
Place these action words on the chart.

Present	Present Continuous	Present Continuous plus helping words *have been*
run		
test		
work		
ride		
laugh		

Practice 10

Choose the correct form of the action word for each sentence below.

1. The airline (lost, is losing) my luggage.

2. According to the schedule, you (will be working, had worked) every Saturday for the next month.

3. I (am watching, have watched) the news every night since the recent events started to unfold. Before that, I (had been watching, watches) only a few nights a week.

4. The instructions (helping, are helping) me through the process.

5. I never (listened, have been listened) to anyone's opinion about my choices.

6. I (worked, working) with computers back in 1990.

7. I used to (sell, have sold) encyclopedias door to door.

8. I (took, have been taking) piano lessons for two months and plan to continue.

Irregular Verbs

Irregular action words/verbs are verbs whose spellings change to a greater degree in order to indicate tense. They are called, *irregular* verbs—for a reason.

Many errors in writing and speaking occur because of these irregular verb changes. Study the list that follows to see if you use the correct forms.

Become familiar with irregular verbs. Use your dictionary or the complete TABE study book to find more irregular verbs.

Present	Past	Future	Past plus helping word *has, have, had*
begin	began	will begin	have begun
bend	bent	will bend	have bent
bet	bet	will bet	have bet
bite	bit	will bite	have bitten
bring	brought	will bring	have brought
buy	bought	will buy	have bought
choose	chose	will choose	have chosen
dive	dived or dove	will dive	have dived
drink	drank	will drink	have drunk
drive	drove	will drive	have driven
fly	flew	will fly	have flown
forbid	forbade	will forbid	have forbidden
forget	forgot	will forget	have forgotten
get	got	will get	have gotten
grind	ground	will grind	have ground
have	had	will have	have had
know	knew	will know	have known
lay (place)	laid	will lay	have laid
lend	lent	will lend	have lent
lie (recline)	lay	will lie	have lain
mistake	mistook	will mistake	have mistaken
run	ran	will run	have run
see	saw	will see	have seen
seek	sought	will seek	have sought

Practice 11

Fill in the blanks below with the correct verb form. These words are not on the list preceeding.

Present	Past	Future	Past plus helping word *has, have, had*
send	_____	will send	_____
shake	_____	_____	have shaken
shine	_____	_____	have shone
shrink	_____	_____	_____
_____	sang	will sing	have sung
slide	_____	will slide	_____
speak	spoke	_____	_____
spin	_____	will spin	_____
take	_____	will take	have taken
tear	tore	_____	_____
think	thought	_____	_____
_____	_____	will throw	have thrown
wake	_____	will wake	_____

Check your answers on page 99 and have all words filled in correctly before you go on to Practice 12.

Practice 12

Choose the correct form of the verb in each sentence. Look back at the list (and your corrected answers to Practice 11) whenever you are in doubt about the correct form to use.

1. I (write/wrote) poetry when I was younger.
2. Amelia has (threw/thrown) her old school papers away.
3. The children have already (wore/worn) out their new clothes.
4. Last summer, I (ran/runned) two miles every morning.
5. I had (brought/brung) in healthy snacks to my daughter's class.
6. Our dog (shaked/shook) his wet fur furiously.
7. We should have (taken/took) the highway to avoid this traffic.
8. Both Maxine and Reid (waked/woke) up late this morning.
9. The child (winded/wound) the propeller on the little red helicopter.
10. Lena and Phil (flew/flown) in this morning.

REVIEW PRACTICE

Practice 13

Practice everything you have learned in Lesson 2. Correct the error in each sentence.

1. Me and my mother send e-mails almost every day.
2. Either you or me will have to make the corrections.
3. Ari, Gwen, and Nancy bowls every Sunday.
4. This store, plus several others in the mall offers coupons in the mall's discount book.
5. Everyone here work hard.
6. Alison be working late tonight.
7. Reggie just joins the community theater.
8. Me and Cal being the first place winner in his school's rap contest.
9. Although we didn't think we would win.
10. Lets be going out tomorrow night to celebrate!

Practice 14

Read the following paragraph. All of the sentences, except one, contain errors. Rewrite them to correct the problems. (Hint: Combine sentences to eliminate the sentence fragment.)

(1) I have learnt a lot about human nature. (2) What people say may not be what they are thinking. (3) Just takes intuition to tell. (4) My friends and me try to help each other. (5) For example, Lindsay's fiancé says, "We'll move to Arizona to be near your family." (6) Then never has time to plan it. (7) She need to ask him the right questions to find out his true intentions.

_____

_____

_____

_____

Answer Key: Section 3, Lesson 2

Practice 1

1. Ray and I left the office at the same time.
2. She and Annie are in the same class.
3. Leslie and he worked on the project together.

4. Val and I met online in a chatroom.

5. Harry and I are stepbrothers.

6. Quincy, Beth, and I are cousins.

7. He and Sonya invited Quincy, Beth, and me to the party.

8. Lorna and I are partners.

Practice 2

1. All new employees must have their forms filled out before the first day of work.

2. Ingrid told the supervisor her e-mail was not working.

3. Each of our children wants a room for himself (or *herself* / or *him or herself*).

   Or

   All of our children want rooms for themselves.

4. Correct as is

5. Anybody who thinks he or she knows everything is sadly mistaken.

6. Rebecca and Tom are both working in their family businesses.

7. Correct as

8. Bill and Calvin are both contributing to the charity from their paycheck.

9. Lorna and I are saving money for a trip.

10. Both Isabelle and Carlos are saving for their retirement years.

Practice 3

1. reserve—is

2. credit card—charges

3. book—is

4. man—needs

5. Brenda—types

6. store—needs (Correct as is)

7. fair—goes

Practice 4

1. are

2. are

3. play

4. writes

5. provides

6. are

7. are

8. tour

Practice 5

1. works
2. matches
3. go
4. offer
5. makes
6. laugh
7. tries
8. are
9. is
10. sells

Practice 6

1. Drew and I share an office.
2. Drew and I share the workload, too.
3. Vic and I go to school together.
4. Lorna's car needs a tune-up.
5. Ethan, Jesse, or Tamara decorates the store for Halloween.
6. Robert and I are engaged.
7. We all go to the gym every morning.
8. Both of us need to be at the meeting.
9. Derek, the manager, and I are working together.
10. Suzanne and I created the slideshow.

Practice 7

(Answers will vary.)

1. I want to talk to you about my resume.
2. My resume and application are enclosed.
3. Return the movies. (Correct as is)
4. The information is enclosed.
5. When the information is enclosed, please seal the envelope.
6. In schools where languages are taught, students have great opportunities to learn about not only language, but also culture.
7. This letter was mailed on Thursday.

8. When money is tight, I can't go out as much.

9. Bring it home. (Correct as is)

10. The airline displays flight information about delays and on-time arrivals and departures.

Practice 8

Answers will vary. Compare this paragraph to your answers. Then review the rules to check your paragraph for proper punctuation and complete sentences.

> We need to discuss what is appropriate to wear for dress down days. What guidelines can we set? Dressing down doesn't mean undressing. We and members of the board are concerned about what clients will think. We don't want to take away dress down days. New guidelines are coming soon.

Practice 9

Part A

call	called	will call	have called
want	wanted	will want	have wanted
walk	walked	will walk	have walked
vote	voted	will vote	have voted
use	used	will use	have used
type	typed	will type	have typed

Part B

run	are running	have been running
test	are testing	have been testing
work	are working	have been working
ride	are riding	have been riding
laugh	are laughing	have been laughing

Practice 10

1. lost
2. will be working
3. have watched, had been watching
4. are helping
5. listened
6. worked
7. sell
8. have been taking

Practice 11

Present	Past	Future	Past plus helping word *has, have, had*
send	sent	will send	have sent
shake	shook	will shake	have shaken
shine	shone	will shine	have shone
shrink	shrank	will shrink	have shrunk
sing	sang	will sing	have sung
slide	slid	will slide	have slid
speak	spoke	will speak	have spoken
spin	spun	will spin	have spun
take	took	will take	have taken
tear	tore	will tear	have torn
think	thought	will think	have thought
throw	threw	will throw	have thrown
wake	woke	will wake	have woken

Practice 12

1. wrote
2. thrown
3. worn
4. ran
5. brought
6. shook
7. taken
8. woke
9. wound
10. flew

REVIEW

Practice 13

1. *My mother and I* send e-mails almost every day.
2. Either you or *I* will have to make the corrections.
3. Ari, Gwen, and Nancy *bowl* every Sunday.
4. This store, plus several others in the mall, *offer* coupons in the mall's discount book.
5. Everyone here *works* hard.
6. Alison *will be* working late tonight.
7. Reggie just *joined* the community theater.

8. Cal and I *are* the first place winner in his school's rap contest.

9. Although we didn't think we would win, *we did.*

10. Let's *go* out tomorrow night to celebrate!

Practice 14

1. I have learned a lot about human nature.

2. What people say may not be what they are thinking. (Correct as is)

3. It just takes intuition to tell.

4. My friends and I try to help each other.

5. & 6. For example, Lindsay's fiancé says, "We'll move to Arizona to be near your family," then never has time to plan it.

7. She needs to ask him the right questions to find out his true intentions.

LESSON 3 More to Know About Verbs

Another Kind of Verb: Linking

Up to now, you have practiced using mostly one kind of verb: an *action* word such as *write, return, plan, arrive, make,* and *look.* The subjects of the sentences *did* something. *Example:* The ballplayer *hits* the ball over the fence.

The *subject,* or *ballplayer,* performed the *action, hit.* Now we will explore another type of verb that does not tell what the subject is doing. This verb tells what the subject was *being.* Some people call these *being verbs* while others refer to them as *nonaction* or *linking verbs. Example:* The other team *was* angry.

You can see that there is no action in the sentence, but there is a description of how the team members *felt*—how they *were.* The verb, *was,* links *team* to the describing word, *angry.*

The most common linking verb is *to be.* Forms of *to be* change based on singular or plural form (number) and tense (time frame).

Linking Verb: To Be

Present	Past	Future	Past with helping words *have, has, had*
I am	was	will be	have been
You are	were	will be	have been
He, she, it is	was	will be	has been
We are	were	will be	have been
They are	were	will be	have been

Notice how *to be* is used to link concepts in the sentences below:

Oscar *is* organized.

Rich *is* a good manager.

I *was* happy for them.

Milo *was* away for two weeks.

Tomorrow *is* my birthday.

What is linked in each sentence? In each one, the subject—Oscar, Rich, I, Milo, Tomorrow—is linked to one of two things: a describing word (*organized, happy, away*) or a word that means the same as or represents the subject (*good manager, my birthday*).

Again, a common error people make when using linking verbs is with agreement:

Karen and me was in the music business.

The above sentence has two errors. The first, of course, is the use of *Me* instead of *I*. The second error is the use of *was* instead of *were* (an agreement error). Because the subject, *Karen and I,* is a plural subject (more than one person in the subject), it requires a plural nonaction verb. Look back at the chart. If you substituted a pronoun for *Karen and I,* the sentence would read:

We were in the music business.

We is a plural subject and *were* is the plural linking verb.

Practice 1

Chose a linking verb in each sentence.

1. Luna (is/are) the fastest runner on our team.

2. We (was/were) very close to a tie.

3. Only one of us (were/was) fast enough to enter the big race. (Hint: Don't be fooled by words between the subject and linking verb.)

4. Walter and Natalie (is/are) coming to the party.

5. This new software version (is/are) easier to learn than the last one.

6. I, along with several of my friends, (was/were) in New Orleans during the big hurricane.

7. Paula and her friends (is/are) taking a cooking class.

8. Liz and her friend, Hiroko, (is/are) meeting me for lunch.

To be is just one example of a linking verb. Now take a look at the longer list below.

Linking Verbs			
are	am	appear	become
is	feel	seem	smell
was	were	grow	taste
be	sound	remain	

Practice 2

Fill each blank with a linking word from the list above. There may be more than one correct choice for some sentences.

1. My customers _____ excited about the new product line.
2. Do you _____ good about the new policy?
3. I'll _____ to be away next weekend.
4. The mocha coffee _____ wonderful!
5. Raul _____ to be a strong manager.
6. The soft rain _____ pretty on the roof.
7. I _____ enjoying the scenery.
8. Do you _____ better today?

Check your answers on page 107 before going on to Practice 3.

Practice 3

What words or phrases does each linking verb in Practice 2 link? Draw an arrow from the subject to the describing word or the word that means the same as the subject. The first one is answered for you below. To complete questions 2–8, write your answers on the exercise below. You should have already checked your answers for Practice 2 before beginning this exercise.

1. My customers are excited about the new product line.

   Answer: customers (subject)   →   excited (descriptive word)

2. →
3. →
4. →
5. →
6. →
7. →
8. →

Practice 4

Read the sentences and decide if they are correct. Change any words that are used incorrectly.

1. These connections are so fast that I never have to wait for pages to open.
2. We was here when the company's doors first opened.
3. The new speakers sounds much stronger than the old ones.
4. Nora, Joan, and Aaron takes the train to work.

5. Either a photograph or more text are needed to fill the extra space in the newsletter.

6. Megan and Mitch is coauthors of a new cookbook.

7. The flower garden is lovely.

8. Harrison's coworkers throwed him a party when he retired.

9. The sales team and their manager is celebrating a record-breaking month.

10. The artists is selling their work in the park this weekend.

Special Forms of Linking Verbs

Linking words are often combined with another word to construct a new word, a *contraction*. In each case, one letter is left out of the combination.

Contraction	Example	Letter Left Out
I'm = I am	I'm almost forty.	a
He's = He is	He's older than I am.	i
She's = She is	She's a good friend.	i
It's = It is	It's time to go.	i
You're = You are	You're always on time.	a
We're = We are	We're running late.	a
They're = They are	They're coming with us.	a

Note: Without the apostrophe, *its* is used to indicate possession.

Example: The town is getting ready for *its* annual fair.

Problems arise when we use a contraction when we should not.
Examples:
There's too many cooks in the kitchen. = *There is too many cooks* in the kitchen.

What is wrong with this sentence? *Cooks* is the subject and it is plural. A plural subject agrees with a plural linking verb. Change *is* to *are*. The construction should be

There are too many *cooks* in the kitchen.

Here's the new flyers. = *Here is* the new flyers.

The above sentences are also *incorrect*. *Flyers* is the subject and it is plural, so you need to use a plural linking verb. Change *is* to *are*. The construction should be

Here *are* the new *flyers*.

A New Wrinkle

What happens when the contraction is negative? Add *not* to the following:

is + not = isn't

are + not = aren't

will + not = won't

were + not = weren't

was + not = wasn't

Never use the contraction, *ain't*. Think about what it takes the place of and use the correct form instead.

Incorrect: I ain't going tonight.

Correct: *I'm* not going tonight.

Or

I am not going tonight.

Even though you will find *ain't* listed in dictionaries as slang, it is not correct usage, ever.

Practice 5

Find the errors in the following sentences. Two are correct as written.

1. Kira isn't going to the beach with us.
2. Wasn't you and Erin revising the database?
3. Ain't you ever going to admit you were wrong?
4. I can't take Saturdays off during the holiday season.
5. My mother always said there's plenty of fish in the sea.
6. There's bound to be days like these.
7. I weren't going to the movies without them.
8. Be careful not to use words that ain't correct usage.

aren't

REVIEW PRACTICE

Practice 6

Read the following paragraphs. Decide if any underlined word is incorrect. Choose the number of the incorrect word. Correct the error.

Paragraph 1

Employers, if (1) they're smart, motivate all employees. Motivation should (2) begin with a positive attitude and positive reinforcement. A manager should tell you what you're doing right and what you're doing wrong; if (3) they're not, how will you know? When a manager (4) criticized, it should be done in a way that instructs and doesn't insult. Good managers (5) know how to teach and inspire.

1. they're
2. begin
3. they're
4. criticized
5. know

Paragraph 2

(1) <u>Are</u> you interested in applying to my company? (2) <u>There's</u> names and numbers I can give you to find out about opportunities. Being referred by me (3) <u>is</u> a big advantage because I'm doing very well there. (4) <u>Doesn't</u> hesitate to use my name. It (5) <u>isn't</u> easy with so much competition, so use any advantage you can.

1. Are
2. There's
3. is
4. Doesn't
5. isn't

Paragraph 3

I just want to be sure that you (1) <u>are</u> serious and ready to commit to the job. They (2) <u>ain't</u> going to respect me if I send them someone who doesn't take the job seriously. (3) <u>I'll</u> be happy to put in a good word for you as long as you assure me you'll give it a chance and (4) <u>won't</u> quit after the first week like you did the last time.

1. are
2. ain't
3. I'll
4. won't

The Time Challenge

In a sentence or a paragraph, the writer needs to keep the time of the verbs consistent.

Example: (1) The scene *is* set. (2) The atmosphere *is* hushed. (3) The curtain *rises* and the audience *applauds.*

Every verb in the brief paragraph above—whether action or linking—is in the same tense.

Sometimes tense will shift within a paragraph, but always check to see that time changes are logical and intentional.

Example: In the past, I *loved* to ski, but now I *prefer* to sit in the lodge by the fire. Next year, I *will go* on a ski trip with friends and *will leave* my skis at home!

Notice that the sentence switches tense, but always with a logical flow. Certain words signal a change in tense, such as: *but now* and *Next year.* Notice the following example, which is *incorrect.*

Example: played guitar for eight years. I *was* in a band and we *play* in small clubs and for private parties. We *play* together, since I was 16.

There are no signal words and there is no sense to the switching of tense. In fact, the switching of tenses in the sentences above is not only confusing, but makes the sentence inaccurate. I *have played* indicates a time in the past that continues into the present and *was in a band* indicates that the band is no longer together. *Was in a band* and *play in small clubs* contradicts itself. *We play together* should, as the opening sentence does, indicate a time continuing into the present: *We have played together.*

Practice 7

Read the paragraphs. Look particularly for inconsistent verb tense. Choose the numbered word (or words) that shows the incorrect verb tense. Correct the error.

Paragraph 1

(1) We <u>decided</u> to buy a used car. (2) Of course, we didn't <u>want</u> to spend too much. (3) It was hard to shop for a used car without <u>knowing</u> car mechanics. (4) Our mechanic <u>offers</u> to help us find a great deal on a safe car. (5) It took a long time to <u>find</u> one we agreed on.

1. decided
2. want
3. knowing
4. offers
5. find

Paragraph 2

(1) We <u>were</u> both insistent on safety. (2) None of the other features <u>were</u> easy to agree upon. (3) To begin with, he <u>wanted</u> a stick shift and I wanted an automatic. (4) Right down to the color, we <u>need</u> different things. (4) What a challenge it <u>was</u> to find a compromise!

1. were
2. were
3. wanted
4. need
5. was

Paragraph 3

(1) We finally <u>found</u> a car we both agreed on and, with a few compromises, we were both happy. (2) To say the least, our mechanic <u>was</u> tired of us, but happy we found one that we liked and wouldn't be back for a while. (3) By this time, we <u>was</u> frustrated, too. (4) It's hard enough to compromise between two people without someone else <u>adding</u> to the pressure to make a decision. (5) It <u>was</u> a big decision we had to make, and I'm glad we took our time!

1. found
2. was
3. was
4. adding
5. was

Answer Key: Section 3, Lesson 3

Practice 1

1. is
2. were
3. was
4. are
5. is
6. was
7. are
8. are

Practice 2

(If you chose any of the choices listed below, you are correct.)

1. are, were, grew, sound, remain
2. feel
3. remain, be
4. is, tastes, smells
5. appears, seems
6. sounds
7. am, was
8. feel

Practice 3

1. customers   →   excited
2. you feel   →   good
3. I'll be   →   away
4. coffee   →   wonderful
5. Raul   →   manager
6. rain   →   pretty
7. I   →   enjoying
8. you   →   better

Practice 4

1. Correct as is.
2. We were here when the company's doors first opened.
3. The new speakers sound much stronger than the old ones.

4. Nora, Joan, and Aaron take the train to work.

5. Either a photograph or more text is needed to fill the extra space in the newsletter.

6. Megan and Mitch are coauthors of a new cookbook.

7. Correct as is.

8. Harrison's coworkers threw him a party when he retired.

9. The sales team and their manager are celebrating a record-breaking month.

10. The artists are selling their work in the park this weekend.

Practice 5

1. Correct as is

2. Weren't

3. Aren't

4. Correct as is

5. there are

6. There are

7. I wasn't

8. aren't

Practice 6

PARAGRAPH 1

4. Replace *criticized* with *criticizes*.

PARAGRAPH 2

2. Replace *There's* with *There are*.

4. Replace *Doesn't* with *Don't*.

PARAGRAPH 3

2. Replace *ain't* with *aren't*.

Practice 7

PARAGRAPH 1

4. Replace *offers* with *offered*.

PARAGRAPH 2

2. Replace *were* with *was*.

4. Replace *need* with *needed*.

PARAGRAPH 3

3. Replace *was* with *were*.

Descriptive Words: Adjectives and Adverbs

A complete sentence requires a subject and action verb.

The girl sings.

Performer = girl   Action = sings

We don't usually write or speak such simple thoughts. We want to describe both the subject and the verb. We accomplish that by adding adjectives and adverbs to sentences.

The young girl sings very beautifully.

Young describes *girl. Beautifully* describes *sings. Very* describes *beautifully.*

With these words, adjectives (*young*) and adverbs (*beautifully* and *very*), the reader has more information.

The adjectives job is to describe or give more information about nouns, or names of people, places, or things.

Examples:

Adjective	Noun
young	girl
older	woman
small	world
red	blouse
fast	car

As you learned in Lesson 3, adjectives also work with linking verbs. A linking verb links the subject of the sentence with a describing word (adjective).

The young girl's voice is beautiful.

Voice is the noun/subject of the sentence and the verb is a linking verb (*is*) instead of an action verb (*sings*). What two words does the linking verb bring together? The answer, of course, is *voice* and *beautiful.*

More examples:

My child is happy.

child (noun) is (linking) happy (adjective describes child)

Your son seems bright.

son (noun) seems (linking verb) bright (adjective describes son)

Practice 1

Now try these sentences on your own. Underline the linking verb and find the subject. Draw an arrow from the adjective to the noun it describes.

1. We are very tired.
2. That job is hard.
3. The children were covered in baking flour.
4. Iris and I are happy to be able to help the cause by handing out pamphlets.

More on Descriptive Words

The job of adverbs is to describe a verb (action word), an adjective, or another adverb.

Examples:
The young girl sings very beautifully.

Beautifully (adverb) describes *sings* (action verb).

Very (adverb) describes *beautifully* (adjective).

Practice 2

Now try these sentences on your own. Draw an arrow from the adverb to the verb it describes. (Hint: Some adverbs describe verbs and others describe other adverbs.)

1. In the neighboring hotel, the band played music too loudly.
2. Lisa and Jack left very early.
3. This sunset shines spectacularly on the ocean.
4. The phone rang loudly and startled Lorna, who was deep in concentration.
5. The baby cried loudly.
6. Today the stars are sparkling brilliantly on this perfectly clear night.
7. Delia sings softly with the radio.

Practice 3

Read the seven sentences above. List the adverbs that describe verbs.

1.
2.
3.
4.
5.
6.
7.

Note: Adverbs that describe verbs most often end in *-ly*. That spelling will become a clue for you when you are trying to decide if a word is an adverb.

The Challenge

The challenge is to use adjectives and adverbs correctly. One common error is confusion between the correct uses of *well* and *good*.

Good vs. Well

Well can be used as an adjective when you talk about health.

I feel *well* again. (*Well* describes *I*.)

At all other times, *well* is an adverb and, as such, describes the action word.

My husband plays guitar *well*. (*Well* describes *plays*.)

Important: *Good* never describes an action. What kind of word does it describe in the next three sentences?

My husband is a good guitar player. (Not, "My husband plays good." *Good* cannot describe the action, *plays*.)

Good describes nouns (people, place, and things).

A *good* book is a great escape.

We live in a *good* neighborhood.

Practice 4

Choose the correct word to complete each sentence.

1. We work (good/well) together.
2. My daughter is not feeling (good/well) today.
3. Aaron is a (good/well) waiter.
4. The car runs (good/well).
5. The new ads have been working (good/well) for us.
6. The story was told (good/well).
7. The offer was a (good/well) one.
8. I don't feel (good/well).

Real vs. Really

Really describes another descriptive word. Did you notice the *-ly*?

Yes, this is an adverb that describes other descriptive words.

It is really hot in here. (*Really* describes the adjective, *hot*.)

Reggie's garden is really lush. (*Really* describes the adjective, *lush*.)

Vera's excuses are really bad. (*Really* describes the adjective, *bad*.)

Real describes a person, place, or thing—a noun.

This is a real opportunity. (*Real* describes the noun, *opportunity.*)

The earrings are real emeralds. (*Real* describes the noun, *emeralds.*)

Although the story was fantasy, the message was very real. (*Real* describes the noun, *message.*)

Practice 5

Choose the correct word in each sentence.

1. The film was (real/really) well done.
2. The eggs were (real/really) too runny for me.
3. The day is (real/really) going too fast!
4. It's (real/really) a perfect day for a picnic.
5. Take a (real/really) break—an extra ten minutes.
6. Take a (real/really) long break.
7. Theo is a (real/really) asset to the team.
8. This band is (real/really) great!

Nice vs. Nicely

This is one of the most common errors in the use of descriptive words.

Nice is an adjective: it describes a person, place, or thing—a noun.

Nicely is an adverb: it describes an action.

The children played nice at the party.

The above sentence is *incorrect.* What does *nice* try to describe? The answer, of course, is *played.* But *nice* cannot describe a verb; *nicely* does.

The children played *nicely* at the party.

If you wanted to describe the children as nice, You would say:

The *nice* children played at the party.

NOT

The *nicely* children played at the party.

Practice 6

Choose the correct word for each sentence.

1. It was such a (nice/nicely) day, I went to the beach.
2. The introductions were presented (nice/nicely).
3. (Nice/Nicely) done!
4. Thelma is really very (nice/nicely).
5. The pictures came out (nice/nicely).
6. Everyone in this restaurant is so (nice/nicely) and friendly.
7. You are so (nice/nicely) dressed today.
8. My niece is a very (nice/nicely) person.

Practice 7

Read the paragraph below. Choose the correct adjective or adverb for each sentence.

(1) Antoine has several (good/well) reasons for moving to Miami. (2) He has a number of (well/good) friends living in Florida and he is more likely to make a professional contact here because this is where he went to school. (3) He also finds it (nice/nicely) to get away from cold New York winters. (4) This move is a (real/really) good opportunity for him to make a fresh start. (5) He feels (good/well) about his prospects. (6) He is also looking forward to spending time with his aunt who lives in Miami and has not been feeling (good/well) for the past several months.

An Important Change

Many adjectives are words of comparison and change form based on *how many* items are being compared and *how* the item is compared.

Akheela runs *fast*.

Gwen runs *faster* than Akheela.

Of all the women in the softball league, Mira runs the *fastest*.

The degree of speed changes the adjective form, but there is more you have to know. When comparing two of anything, most adjectives end in *-er*. When comparing more than two, add *-est* to the adjective to represent the least or the most.

Adjective	Comparison of Two	Comparison of More Than Two
fast	faster	fastest
green	greener	greenest
blue	bluer	bluest
pretty	prettier	prettiest

Trouble Ahead

We tend to run into trouble with comparisons in two ways: (1) Sometimes adjectives change spelling in ways other than the addition of *-er* or *-est* to the base word. (2) Some describing words are too long and become awkward when we place an extra syllable on the end. Consider this:

That is the *advancedest* course in our program.

Because *advanced* is a three-syllable word and because it becomes a very awkward word, you must not use *-er* or *-est*. Instead, add *more* or *most* and keep the base word, *advanced*.

That course is the *most advanced* in our program.

(The sentence indicates a comparison among three or more courses. The word *most* is used instead of adding *-est*.)

Or

That course is *more advanced* than the one I took last semester.

(The sentence indicates a comparison between two courses. The word *more* is used instead of adding *-er*.)

We sometimes, mistakenly, use *more* or *most* plus the *-er* or *-est* ending and that is too much of a good thing.

Each news story was *more scarier* than the last.

Corrected:

Each news story was *scarier* than the last.

Here are some other words that need to use *more* and *most* in comparisons.

Adjective	Comparison of Two	Comparison of More than Two
enormous	more enormous	most enormous
difficult	more difficult	most difficult
beautiful	more beautiful	most beautiful
valuable	more valuable	most valuable
wonderful	more wonderful	most wonderful

Some adjectives are spelled entirely differently when they are used to compare two or more things. Look at the chart below.

Adjective	Comparison of Two	Comparison of More than Two
good	better	best
bad	worse	worst

What's wrong with this sentence?

That was the *worse* show I've ever seen.

We can assume that the writer has seen more than two shows. How would you correct the sentence?

That was the *worst* show I've ever seen.

Try this:

This class is the *better* of the three offered.

Corrected:

This class is the *best* of the three offered.

REVIEW PRACTICE

Practice 8

Find an error in all but one of these sentences. Write a correction in the space provided.

1. We have the bestest seats in the theater. _____

2. Each contestant was worse than the last. _____

3. Sandra runs quicker than Steve. _____

4. This is the worse song on the CD. _____

5. You'll never find a wonderfuller friend than Michael. _____

6. The test will be more easier if we study. _____

7. Lilly is always the more beautifully dressed person of everyone in our office. _____

8. I feel more better than yesterday. _____

9. Camille lives closest to me than Ronald. _____

10. Sally is a happiest person. _____

11. This job is more better than my last. _____

12. Valerie is the better cook of the group. _____

13. Lena plays the drums good. _____

14. Your friends are more opener than mine. _____

15. The band played nice tonight. _____

16. The band played good. _____

Prepositions

Occasionally, we need more than a single word to add meaning to a sentence. We add a phrase instead. Example:

Children played *in the park.*

The phrase, *in the park,* describes where the children played. The entire phrase acts as a descriptive word. In this case, it describes *played,* the verb, so it acts as an adverb. As you will see, descriptive phrases frequently come between the subject and verb.

A *summary* of all the chapters *is* in the last part of the book.

There is a practical reason for being able to recognize descriptive phrases. It will help you recognize the subject. In the above sentence, the word *chapters* is a part of the descriptive phrase and is not the subject. The sentence below shows *chapters* as the subject. (Note that the verb becomes plural to agree with the plural subject.)

The *chapters are* summarized at the end of the book.

Try this one:

The waiters at the restaurant (work/works) late.

Hint: Remove the phrase first. What is the action verb? The answer is *works.* Who works? The *waiters.* That is the subject. Is the subject singular or plural? The answer is plural. Which word should you choose? *Waiters work.*

A group of words that typically start descriptive phrases are called *prepositions.* The phrases they start are called *prepositional phrases.* All of the phrases you have worked with so far in this section are prepositional phrases. Look back at the first word of each example sentence. They are called prepositions and they are listed below.

Prepositions					
after	at	along	alongside	among	around
before	beside	between	by	except	for
from	in	into	of	off	on
over	to	through	under	up	with

Practice 9

In the sentences below, you will find descriptive prepositional phrases. Each starts with one of the prepositions in the list. Underline the phrases. Then find the subject and the verb. Place an *S* over the subject and a *V* over the verb.

1. The change fell through the whole in his pocket.
2. We are all among friends here.
3. I keep an umbrella in the car.
4. Kira keeps a notebook beside the bed.
5. I didn't see any rest stops between here and there.
6. Everything I have fits into a small storage compartment.
7. This gift from Joseph was very generous.
8. The parents are divided in their thinking.

Warning!
A descriptive or prepositional phrase should take its place next to the word it describes.

When prepositional phrases are misplaced, confusion results. Example:
The supervisor yelled to his assistant on call.

Who was on call, the supervisor or his assistant? You cannot say for sure after reading this sentence. Rewrite it:
The supervisor on call yelled to his assistant.

Practice 10

Find the incorrectly placed prepositional phrases in these sentences. Rewrite the sentences and place the phrases closer to the words they describe. If you have trouble recognizing the prepositions, look back to the list given above.

1. The bag belongs to that man walking the dog in the yellow jacket.

   _____

2. The actors played angels who were sent from heaven in the movie.

   _____

3. I hung on the wall a picture of you.

_____

4. Because she drank too much coffee, Mabel couldn't sleep in the morning all night.

_____

5. On the table, the business representatives put their brochures out.

_____

6. The children went swimming with their mothers in the pool.

_____

7. The flowers planted by Esther and Doris look lovely in the pot.

_____

8. About two thieves who rob a bank, Brenda and Maury wrote a book.

_____

Answer Key: Section 3, Lesson 4

Practice 1

1. We <u>are</u> very tired. (subject is _We, tired_ describes _We_)
2. The job <u>is</u> hard. (subject is _job, hard_ describes _job_)
3. The children <u>were</u> covered in baking flour. (subject is _children, covered_ describes _children_)
4. Iris and I <u>are</u> happy to be able to help the cause by handing out pamphlets. (subject is _Iris and I, happy_ describes _Iris and I_)

Practice 2

1. adverb: _loudly_—describes _played_; adverb: _too_—describes _loudly_
2. adverb: _early_—describes _left_; adverb: _very_—describes _early_
3. adverb: _spectacularly_—describes _shines_
4. adverb: _loudly_—describes _rang_
5. adverb: _loudly_—describes _cried_
6. adverb: _brilliantly_—describes _sparkling_; adverb: _perfectly_—describes _clear_
7. adverb: _softly_—describes _sings_

Practice 3

1. loudly
2. early
3. spectacularly

4. loudly
5. loudly
6. brilliantly
7. softly

Practice 4

1. well
2. well
3. good
4. well
5. well
6. well
7. good
8. well

Practice 5

1. really
2. really
3. really
4. really
5. real
6. really
7. real
8. really

Practice 6

1. nice
2. nicely
3. Nicely
4. nice
5. nicely
6. nice
7. nicely
8. nice

Practice 7

1. good
2. good

3. nice
4. really
5. good
6. well

Practice 8

1. best
2. correct as is
3. faster *or* more quickly
4. worst
5. more wonderful
6. easier
7. most beautifully
8. better
9. closer
10. correct as is
11. better
12. best
13. well
14. more open
15. nicely
16. well

Practice 9

1. The **change** (subject) **fell** (verb) <u>through the whole in his pocket.</u> (prepositional phrase)
2. **We** (subject) **are** (verb) all <u>among friends</u> (prepositional phrase) here.
3. **I** (subject) **keep** (verb) an umbrella <u>in the car.</u> (prepositional phrase)
4. **Kira** (subject) **keeps** (verb) a notebook <u>beside the bed.</u> (prepositional phrase)
5. **I** (subject) didn't **see** (verb) any rest stops <u>between here and there.</u> (prepositional phrase)
6. **Everything** (subject) I have **fits** (verb) <u>into a small storage compartment.</u> (prepositional phrase)
7. This **gift** (subject) <u>from Joseph</u> (prepositional phrase) **was** (verb) very generous.
8. The **parents** (subject) **are** (verb) divided <u>in their thinking.</u> (prepositional phrase)

Practice 10

1. The bag belongs to that man in the yellow jacket who is walking the dog.
2. The actors in the movie played angels who were sent from heaven.
3. I hung a picture of you on the wall.
4. Because she drank too much coffee in the morning, Mabel couldn't sleep all night.
5. The business representatives put their brochures out on the table.
6. The children went swimming in the pool with their mothers.
7. The flowers planted in the pot by Esther and Doris look lovely.
8. Brenda and Maury wrote a book about two thieves who rob a bank.

LESSON 5 Punctuation

Why Do We Need Punctuation?

For the most part, the use of punctuation is logical. Without punctuation, clarity would be lost. We avoid run-on sentences, for example, by using a period or a semicolon.

Example of a run-on sentence:

I work in a hospital I have worked there eight years I enjoy helping people.

Possible corrections:

I work in a hospital. I have worked there eight years. I enjoy helping people.

I work in a hospital. I have worked there for eight years; I enjoy helping people.

End Marks

The period (.), question mark (?), and exclamation mark (!) are all end marks. They are the most common and the most easily used punctuation marks. Without the use of end marks and capital letters, all would be chaos.

Example:
Roger's father is a lawyer and wanted his son to follow in his footsteps and go to law school Roger has his own dreams he wants to become a chef he's been interested in cooking for some time vegetarian dishes are his specialty everyone loves his cooking cooking school is his dream

STUDY TIP
Here is a list of capitalization rules. Refer to this whenever you are unsure about using a capital letter.

Capitalize:

- The first word in a sentence
- The first word of a direct quotation

- The word *I*
- Place names, people's names, organization names, specific course names, languages
- A title when it is a form of address: Lieutenant George Grant.
- Names of important historical events and ages (World War II, Declaration of Independence)
- The title of a book, play, magazine, or poem (just the first and important words in each, e.g., *Of Mice and Men*)
- Sections of the country, not directions. Examples: I had lived in the East for many years. Turn east onto Broad Street
- Days of the week, months, and holidays

Practice 1

In the following paragraphs, place end marks and capital letters where they are needed. Do not worry about commas or any other punctuation marks.

1. this filing system is a terrible mess I can't tell what's new or old I can't even find files alphabetically, and one computer has a document with changes that are not in the same document on another computer the printed versions could match what's in any computer or none at all I give up

2. the new office is going to be old-fashioned, furnished with antiques the boss, Susie Que, wants to be unique and get away from the sleek, modern look of the typical office she used to be an antiques dealer and knows how to find great deals on unique pieces the equipment will be ultra-modern, but the furnishings will be wood instead of metal Susie hopes to create a warm, friendly atmosphere

3. I was recruited by my boss to evaluate the company website and suggest ways to update and improve I only halfheartedly agreed because I know my input will be filed in a drawer for a year as it was the last time that website has needed an overhaul for years

Practice 2

For each numbered word(s), select the correct option. Look for errors in punctuation and capitalization.

1. Howard moved to <u>Brooklyn Tracy</u> took over his job.

   A Insert a comma after *Brooklyn.*

   B Insert a question mark after *job.*

   C Insert an exclamation point instead of a period.

   D Insert a period after *Brooklyn.*

   E Correct as is.

2. We'll meet at <u>universe cafe</u> for lunch.

   A Insert a period after *Universe*

   B Insert capitals *U* and *C* on *universe cafe*

   C Insert a comma between *universe* and *cafe*

   D Insert an exclamation point at the end of the sentence

   E Correct as is

3. Check with me before you call the board <u>president it</u> is important for us to make our case together.

   A Insert capital *I* on *it*

   B Insert capital *P* on *president.*

   C Insert a question mark after *president*

   D Insert a period after *president* and capitalize *It*

   E Correct as is

4. Because of the storm, the outdoor film feature is <u>cancelled read</u> the flyer to see if they scheduled a rain date.

   A Insert a capital *F* on *film*

   B Insert a comma and capital *R*

   C Delete the word *see*

   D Insert a period after *cancelled* and capitalize *Read*

   E Correct as is

5. I love summer <u>rains don't</u> you?

   A Insert a comma after *rains* and capitalize *Don't*

   B Insert a period after *rains* and capitalize *Don't*

   C Insert a question mark

   D Insert an exclamation mark

   E Correct as is

6. We are moving to Phoenix in <u>april I'm</u> so excited

   A April. I'm so excited!

   B April, I'm so excited!

   C April. I'm so excited:

   D April! I'm so excited,

   E Correct as is

7. My brother goes to school down <u>south</u> at <u>georgia state university</u>.

    A south at Georgia State University

    B South at Georgia State University

    C South at Georgia State university

    D south at georgia state University

    E Correct as is

Commas

Commas are meant to clarify meaning. Read the paragraph below. Where would you insert commas?

> Commas can be confusing. They are often over-used and many people think they should be inserted wherever a speaker would take a breath. Then again commas are also often left out where they belong. Though they are confusing there is hope. Learning some basic punctuation rules will keep you from guessing where commas go so that you can use them confidently. The rules do however take some effort to learn. Take your time with this section and as always check your answers to each practice before you go forward.

The following checklist will help you to understand the correct uses of commas and to correct any errors you may have missed in the sample paragraph.

Comma Rules

1. Use a comma after a salutation in a friendly letter.
Dear Charles,

2. Use a comma after the closing in a business or friendly letter.
Sincerely,

Ingrid

3. Separate items in a series with commas.
We find leads, call prospects, and make sales.
(The last comma in the series is optional unless it clarifies meaning.)

4. Use a comma to separate an introductory phrase from the complete thought.
On rainy Saturdays, I catch up on work.

STUDY TIP
Take a careful look at this example. Writers sometimes make the error of thinking that the introductory words (On rainy Saturdays) represent a sentence, but it is only a fragment. Don't fall into the sentence fragment trap!

5. Insert commas to separate words that interrupt the flow of the sentence.
Justin, though he doesn't know it yet, is next in line for a promotion.

STUDY TIP

How can you tell which words interrupt the flow of the sentence? Eliminating them will not affect the sentence's meaning.

Justin is next in line for a promotion.

6. Commas set off the words *however, nevertheless, inasmuch as, therefore,* when they interrupt a complete thought.

   Heather, however, is not performing well on her team evaluations.

7. A comma separates two complete thoughts that are joined by a connecting word such as *but, for, or, and.*

   We are looking for new office space, and we are considering moving into the city.

8. Use commas to separate more than one descriptive word describing the same word.

   Our school's mascot is a big, blue kangaroo.

9. Insert a comma to separate the name of a city from the name of a state or country.

   Sedona, Arizona

10. Insert a comma to separate a direct quotation from the rest of the sentence.

    Examples:

    "I can assist you in any way you need," Tom offered.

    He shouted into his cell phone, "I can't hear you!"

    "I have seen your work," Olivia said, "so I am confident you're the right person for the job."

11. Insert a comma between the day and the year and between the year and the rest of the sentence.

    I was married on June 14, 2006, in a small ceremony on the beach.

Practice 3

Insert commas where they are needed.

Pauline owns a clothing store downtown a few blocks from the tourist areas that always carries the newest styles. She and her friend Wendy opened the store 15 years ago and they have been doing very well. They offer quality items friendly service and fashion advice. I recommend the store to everyone who comes to town. In fact all the locals recommend it to tourists.

Practice 4

Insert or remove commas wherever necessary.

What, can we do within our community to help the hurricane victims? The city set up shelters and we are all donating food clothing and other necessities. Even the children want to help and by denoting some of their toys.

Practice 5

For questions 1–5, decide if the underlined parts need correction. Write the correction or *correct as is* on the line provided.

1. What do you know about alternative healing<u>.</u>

   _____

2. Believe it or <u>not many</u> people get well without taking traditional medicine<u>?</u>

   _____

3. Some people see herbs as a last <u>resort, others</u> try them first.

   _____

4. Some <u>people, prefer</u> other alternatives, such as acupuncture.

   _____

5. If medication is giving you side effects<u>,</u> why not try talking to a natural doctor?

   _____

Use Commas Logically

Do not insert commas where they are not needed. Avoid the following common overuses of commas.

1. Do not use a comma before *but, for,* or *and* unless both parts of the separated sentence have one subject/performer.

   Incorrect: <u>I adopted</u> a new kitten, and <u>took</u> him for shots immediately.

   Correct: <u>I adopted</u> a new kitten and <u>took</u> him for shots immediately.

2. When a sentence starts with a complete thought, do not use a comma to separate it from the incomplete thought that follows.

   Incorrect: Time always goes too fast, when I'm on vacation.

   Correct: Time always goes too fast when I'm on vacation.

Reminder: You can see that the subject of commas frequently brings up the subject of sentence fragments. Keep this in mind as you work through the review exercise.

REVIEW PRACTICE

Practice 6

Find and correct errors in capitalization, end marks, and comma usage.

1. my boss asked me to fill out a self assessment
2. after the morning meeting my boss took me aside and asked me what I thought.

3. dear duncan

   thank you for meeting with me. it was a pleasure and i look forward to speaking with you after you have had time to review the proposal.

   Sincerely

   Suzette

4. Carla finished the report spell checked it and submitted it

5. After working here for 10 years I'm ready for a change.

6. It seems like the new computers just arrived and they are already out of date.

7. Ursula as acting manager has called a morning meeting.

8. I have been a lifeguard at our community pool for the past four years this will be my last summer.

9. Nichole's twins were born on September 20 2005.

10. I don't know why we couldn't get this delivery scheduled for Thursday?

11. "I am not interested" she replied thank you anyway.

12. Is this going to be an outdoor or indoor event.

13. Jack is a warm caring person.

14. The story alice in wonderland is a classic.

15. "The weather reporter said: It's going to be a warm sunny day out there."

Semicolons

A semicolon is stronger than a comma; it is, actually, more like a period. It separates two complete, related sentences. Instead of a period, the semicolon combines two otherwise complete sentences to express the close relationship between two thoughts.

   Example:

The e-mail will be forwarded to every department; let's proofread one more time.

The semicolon is one option for separating complete thoughts.

Options for separating complete thoughts:

1. **Comma plus a small connecting word, such as** *so, for, but, and, or, nor*
   Example: I just got my degree, and I am an engineer.

2. **End mark**
   Example: I just got my degree. I am an engineer.

3. **Semicolon**
   Example: I just got my degree; I am an engineer.

4. **Semicolon plus a transition word such as** *however, therefore, nevertheless, inasmuch as* **(Notice that the transition word is then followed by a comma.)**

   Example: I just got my engineering degree; however, it's hard to find a job.

Additional Uses for Semicolons

1. A complex sentence might require a semicolon instead of a comma. If a sentence has a number of commas, the additional comma to separate complete thoughts could cause confusion. In this case, make the separation stand out by using a semicolon instead of a comma.

   Example: I just got my engineering degree on May 18, 2006, from Phoenix, Arizona; but it's hard to find a job.

2. As you know, commas separate items in a list (eggs, butter, soy milk). But what happens when those items have commas within the list? Again, the semicolon comes to the rescue and keeps us from being confused by too many commas.

   Example: The committee included: Ray Stark, of Bradbush Industries; Perlina Patel, of Tradestar International; and Ricky Mansfield, freelance agent, also representing the Universe Cooperative.

REVIEW PRACTICE

Practice 7

Insert commas, end marks, and semicolons wherever they are needed. Look for run-on sentences and correct them.

1. I am very tired I work too late every night.
2. I'll be ready to talk after lunch please call any time after 2:00.
3. Justin my brother said that he has extra tickets for the game.
4. Wanda said "I want to congratulate you."
5. We just refinished our house therefore we cannot afford to take a summer vacation.
6. The Petersons grow tomatoes beets and lettuce.
7. On your way to the meeting please pick up bagels.
8. I love my job I feel good about the work I do.
9. I have been at this job for nine years however no one seems to notice the extra work I do.
10. I want to thank my brother Howard for his support and encouragement my best friend Jacob for always being there for me and most of all my parents for their loving guidance.

Quotation Marks

You have had some experience working with commas and quotation marks. Quotation marks are used to set off the exact words said by a person.

Direct quotation: Molly said, "I need your help."

Indirect quotation: Molly said that she needs your help.

One word, *that,* changes the direct quotation to an indirect one. The word *that* turns the statement into a *report* of what Molly said.

To use quotation marks correctly, you need to know a number of rules.

Quotation Mark Rules

1. Use quotation marks to indicate the exact words of a speaker. Important: Periods and commas are always inside the quotation marks.

   Example: "Humor is mankind's greatest blessing."

2. Quotation marks, unless they begin a sentence, should be preceded by a colon or a comma.

   Examples:

   Mark Twain said: "Humor is mankind's greatest blessing."

   Or

   Mark Twain said, "Humor is mankind's greatest blessing."

3. Some quotations are interrupted. When the sentence continues from one set of quotations to the next, the second part begins with a small letter, not a capital.

   Example: "Humor," said Mark Twain, "is mankind's greatest blessing."

   When the second part of the quotation begins with a new sentence, begin as you would all new sentences, with a capital letter.

   Example: "Age is an issue of mind over matter," said Mark Twain, "If you don't mind, it doesn't matter."

4. Place a semicolon after closing quotation marks.

   Example: Twain called humor "mankind's greatest blessing"; and I agree.

5. If the entire sentence is a question, but the quotation is not, place the question mark after the closing quotation marks. (The same rule applies for the exclamation mark.)

   Example 1: Did Tommy say, "Meet me there at 6:00"?

   Example 2: He even said, "I'll be there early"!

   If the quotation is a question but the sentence is not, place the question mark inside the quotation marks. (Again, the same applies to the exclamation mark.)

Example 1: Holden asked, "Where do the ducks go in winter?"

Example 2: Paulo shouted, "I'm not shouting!"

Note: Never use two forms of punctuation at the end of a quotation. Use logic to decide where question marks and exclamation marks should be placed.

6. Use quotation marks to enclose titles of poems, chapters, articles, or any part of a book or magazine. (Remember the comma rule: When the title is followed by a comma, place the comma inside the quotation marks.) Note: Italics are often used—and are perfectly acceptable—in place of quotation marks.

   Example: "Ode to My Socks," by Pablo Neruda, was written in honor of a new pair of wool socks.

7. Use single quotation marks for a quotation within a quotation.

   Example: "I remember very clearly that you said, 'The report will be on your desk in the morning,' and I don't see a report on my desk!"

Practice 8

Correct and punctuate these sentences. Add capital letters where necessary.

1. Steffen said that the store manager is coming and the store has to look perfect
2. Steffen said the store manager is coming and the store has to look perfect
3. Debbie and Donna asked what time the manager would be coming in
4. Debbie asked what time is the manager coming in
5. Why didn't Debbie just start cleaning up
6. Steffen shouted the manager is on her way
7. The manager is on her way said Steffen we'd better move quickly

REVIEW PRACTICE

Practice 9

Correct and Punctuate these sentences. Add capital letters where necessary.

1. "I don't mind a summer shower she said
2. She said, we can bring the party inside if it rains."
3. The weatherman said that we would have clear skies
4. I would like to work for them would you
5. "If you are tired" I said "let me drive
6. After reading the article, "The Happy Customer" I had a better understanding of how to appeal to customers

7. After you enter the new data remember to back up the files she instructed

8. Did you say "Brandon was fired"

9. "Did you know that" Yolanda asked

10. "Get out of my garden" Conrad shouted at the bunnies.

More Punctuation: Colon, Hyphen, Apostrophe, Dash, Parentheses, and Brackets

Study the rules below, and then try the practice exercise.

1. **The Colon**

   Use a colon to introduce a list.

   Example: Please see that the meeting room is equipped with the following: a flip chart, magic markers, and masking tape.

   Use a colon after the salutation in a business letter.

   Example: Dear Mr. Johnson:

   Use a colon between numbers that show time.

   Example: Please be at your desk by 8:30.

2. **The Hyphen**

   Use a hyphen to divide a word at the end of a line. Always divide words between syllables.

   Example: Online dictionaries and encyclopedias are extreme-ly convenient.

   Use a hyphen to divide compound numbers from twenty-one to ninety-nine.

   Examples: forty-two, twenty-three, eighty-seven

   Use a hyphen when you add some prefixes or when you add self to another word.

   Examples:
   non-native   self-respect

   ex-partner   self-reliant

3. **The Apostrophe**

   Use an apostrophe to show that one or more letters have been left out of a word (a contraction).

   Examples:
   Laura isn't (is not) working here anymore.

   I'll (I will) call you when we're (we are) on our way.

   It's (It is) not too late to make the necessary changes.

Use an apostrophe to show possession. (a) Place the apostrophe before the *s* in singular words. (b) Place the apostrophe after the *s* in plural words. (c) Some words become plural by other spelling changes.

Examples:

Singular	Plural
the bird's song	the birds' song
the woman's apartment	the women's apartment
the baby's cries	the babies' cries
the child's game	the children's game
Names follow the same rules.	
Ms. Davidson's car	The Davidsons' property
Ms. Jones's class	The Joneses' property

Use an apostrophe to show the plural of letters and numbers.

Examples:

Start the game with the 1's in the top row.

Z's are worth the most points in Scrabble.

STUDY TIP

Don't use an apostrophe in a possessive pronoun: theirs, its, hers, whose.

Examples:
The beach blanket is theirs.
The kite lost its tail.
The red bag is hers.
Whose is this?

4. **The Dash**

Use dashes to mark an important interruption in the sentence.

Example: Your photograph—as colorful as it is—must be submitted to the contest in black and white.

Use a dash to sum up previous words.

Example: Beautiful weather, nowhere to be, and good friends—that is my idea of the perfect Sunday.

5. **Parentheses**

Words in parentheses are not directly related to the main thought of the sentence. They are an *aside* or an *addition* not absolutely necessary to the thought.

Example: Jenna backs up her computer every night (onto a Lacie backup hard drive).

Practice 10

Choose the correct word and punctuation in the parentheses.

1. (Its/It's) time to go home.
2. My son gets along well with his (ex wife/ex-wife).

3. When I was (twenty two/**twenty-two**), I started my online business.

4. Terrance started the letter, Dear Mr. (**Murray,**/Murray:).

5. We were picked up (**—in a limousine—** / —in a limousine) for the concert.

6. Frieda joined a (woman's/**women's**) business organization.

7. Ned, (whose new with the company / **who's new with the company**), was quiet at the meeting.

8. I learned a lot in (**Ms. Brown's class** / Ms. Browns' class).

Answer Key: Section 3, Lesson 5

Practice 1

1. This filing system is a terrible mess. I can't tell what's new or old. I can't even find files alphabetically, and one computer has a document with changes that are not in the same document on another computer. The printed versions could match what's in any computer or none at all. I give up!

2. The new office is going to be old-fashioned, furnished with antiques. The boss, Susie Que, wants to be unique and get away from the sleek, modern look of the typical office. She used to be an antique dealer and knows how to find great deals on unique pieces. The equipment will be ultra-modern, but the furnishings will be wood instead of metal. Susie hopes to create a warm, friendly atmosphere.

3. I was recruited by my boss to evaluate the company website and suggest ways to update and improve. I only halfheartedly agreed because I know my input will be filed in a drawer for a year as it was the last time. That website has needed an overhaul for years.

Practice 2

1. D
2. B
3. D
4. D
5. B
6. A
7. B

Practice 3

Pauline owns a clothing store downtown, a few blocks from the tourist areas that always carries the newest styles. She and her friend, Wendy, opened the store 15 years ago, and they have been doing very well. They offer quality items, friendly service, and fashion advice. I recommend the store to everyone who comes to town. In fact, all the locals recommend it to tourists.

Practice 4

What can we do, within our community, to help the hurricane victims? The city set up shelters, and we are all donating food, clothing, and other necessities. Even the children want to help by donating some of their toys.

Practice 5

1. healing?
2. not, many/medicine.
3. resort. Others
4. people prefer
5. Correct as is

Practice 6

1. My boss asked me to fill out a self-assessment.
2. After the morning meeting, my boss took me aside and asked me what I thought.
3. Dear Duncan:

   Thank you for meeting with me. It was a pleasure, and I look forward to speaking with you after you have had time to review the proposal.

   Sincerely,

   Suzette
4. Carla finished the report, spell-checked it, and submitted it.
5. After working here for 10 years, I'm ready for a change.
6. It seems like the new computers just arrived, and they are already out of date.
7. Ursula, as acting manager, has called a morning meeting.
8. I have been a lifeguard at our community pool for the past four years; this will be my last summer.
9. Nichole's twins were born on September 20, 2005.
10. I don't know why we couldn't get this delivery scheduled for Thursday.
11. "I am not interested," she replied. "Thank you anyway."
12. Is this going to be an outdoor or indoor event?
13. Jack is a warm, caring person.
14. The story, "Alice in Wonderland," is a classic.
15. The weather reporter said, "It's going to be a warm, sunny day out there."

Practice 7

Answers may vary as some have several options. If your answer differs from one below double check it against the rules in this lesson.

1. I am very tired; I work too late every night.

   Or

   I am very tired. I work too late every night.

2. I'll be ready to talk after lunch. Please call any time after 2:00.

   Or

   I'll be ready to talk after lunch; please call any time after 2:00.

3. Justin, my brother, said that he has extra tickets for the game.

4. Wanda said, "I want to congratulate you."

5. We just refinished our house; therefore, we cannot afford to take a summer vacation.

   Or

   We just refinished our house. Therefore, we cannot afford to take a summer vacation.

6. The Petersons grow tomatoes, beets and lettuce.

   Or

   The Petersons grow tomatoes, beets, and lettuce.

7. On your way to the meeting, please pick up bagels.

8. I love my job; I feel good about the work I do.

   Or

   I love my job. I feel good about the work I do.

9. I have been at this job for nine years; however, no one seems to notice the extra work I do.

   Or

   I have been at this job for nine years. However, no one seems to notice the extra work I do.

10. I want to thank my brother, Howard, for his support and encouragement; my best friend, Jacob, for always being there for me; and, most of all, my parents for their loving guidance.

REVIEW

Practice 8

1. Steffen said that store manager is coming, and the store has to look perfect.
2. Steffen said, "The store manager is coming, and the store has to look perfect."

3. Debbie and Donna asked what time the manager would be coming in.
4. Debbie asked, "What time is the manager coming in?"
5. Why didn't Debbie just start cleaning up?
6. Steffen shouted, "The manager is on her way!"
7. "The manager is on her way," said Steffen, "We'd better move quickly."

Practice 9

1. "I don't mind a summer shower," she said.
2. She said, "We can bring the party inside if it rains."
3. The weatherman said that we would have clear skies.
4. I would like to work for them. Would you?
5. "If you are tired," I said, "let me drive."
6. After reading the article, "The Happy Customer," I had a better understanding of how to appeal to customers.
7. "After you enter the new data, remember to back up the files," she instructed.
8. Did you say that "Brandon was fired"?
9. "Did you know that?" Yolanda asked.
10. "Get out of my garden!" Conrad shouted at the bunnies.

Practice 10

1. It's
2. ex-wife
3. twenty-two
4. Murray:
5. —in a limousine—
6. women's
7. who's new with the company
8. Ms. Brown's class

LESSON 6 Constructing Sentences and Paragraphs

Decide if the words and thoughts are parallel. Each part of the sentence should be expressed in the same grammatical form.

Example: Write your report honestly, and record the facts in a succinct way.

In the first half of the sentence, the writer instructs you to report *honestly* (an adverb describing write). In the second half of the sentence, you are told to report the facts in a succinct way. How can you change that prepositional phrase (in a succinct way) to match the *–ly* adverb, *honestly*?

The answer is to change the phrase to one word: *succinctly.* Now the sentence is parallel.

Correction: Write your report honestly and succinctly.

Practice 1

Correct any punctuation errors in these sentences and rewrite the sentences so that they are parallel.

1. My new suit is simple, stylish, and looks professional.
2. I worked late every night this week, because two people in the department were being sick.
3. We both like to walk on the beach and riding on the bike path.
4. The book was clear informative; and written well.
5. My favorite team sports are football, softball, and to play volleyball.
6. Henry is not only a good friend but is being a great boss.
7. My doctor gives me advice on relaxation, nutrition, and what kinds of exercise I should do.
8. Ron plays guitar, Rocky sings, and I am playing the drums.
9. The supervisor wrote the incident report clearly, promptly, and was quite fair.
10. Julianne is fair and conducts business in an honest manner.
11. Meditation is both relaxing and makes me feel at peace.

Combining Ideas

Good writing is simple and direct; however, certain writing techniques make sentences more interesting and meaningful. The punctuation you have studied, plus connecting words, will help you create better sentences and paragraphs. Read this paragraph:

> *Example:* I went for an interview this morning. The office was undecorated. The walls were white. Lightbulbs hung uncovered from the ceiling. The furniture was covered in dust. Even the walls were dirty. I saw a mouse run across the floor. That was the last straw. I would never work there!

In the above paragraph, there are no errors that we can point to. Still, there are ways to improve the flow of ideas by combining them. Read the following possible corrections to get a feel for the kinds of changes that improve a paragraph.

Possible corrections:

1. I went for an interview this morning. The office was stark, with undecorated, white walls and uncovered lightbulbs hanging from the ceiling. The furniture was covered in dust; even the walls were dirty. When I saw a mouse run across the floor, that was the last straw. I would never work there!

2. I went for an interview this morning, and the office was undecorated; it had uncovered lightbulbs hanging from the ceiling and stark, white walls. The furniture was covered in dust, and even the walls were dirty. I saw a mouse run across the floor; that was the last straw. I would never work there!

3. I went for an interview this morning in a dusty, undecorated office with dirty, white walls and lightbulbs hanging, uncovered, from the ceiling. When I saw a mouse run across the floor, it was the last straw. I would never work there!

Signals for Combining Sentences:

1. Does it contain scattered, descriptive information? Can (and should) that information be put into one sentence?
2. When a sentence begins with *It was, It is,* or *This is,* ask yourself how you might join the sentence with the one before or how you might change the word order to make a stronger sentence.

Combining sentences sometimes requires that you make one part less important than the other. Logically, this is called subordination. First, decide on your emphasis. Look at the following example:

Example: After I saw the mouse running through the dust, I knew I would never work there!

The complete thought that comes after the comma receives the greater emphasis. True of many sentences in general, the final words receive the emphasis. The subordinating (supporting) thought comes after a subordinating signal word: *after.*

Subordinating words are important to know about. Below are some examples:

Subordinating Words			
after	if	though	
as	because	unless	therefore
when	since	where	whereas

Practice 2

Combine the sentences below, subordinating one part of the sentence to the other. Choose a subordinating word from the list above. Insert the appropriate punctuation.

1. The film festival will be running all week. I don't care if we miss the opening night.
2. I got a new cell phone plan. I found one that offers more minutes.
3. I sent in the nomination. It's late and may not be considered.
4. I called for service this morning. No one has called back yet.

5. I won't use that color. I won't use it if you don't like it.
6. My boss screams all the time. I am looking for a new job.
7. I want to work at the clinic. I can help people.
8. This tea tastes terrible. The water here isn't clean.

You have also learned about using commas or semicolons to connect sentences to *connect* or *transition* ideas. This section offers a more complete list of transition words and additional practice. Below is a list of words used with commas and semicolons.

Words that Link Equal Ideas			
and	also	nor	
or	however	but	besides
yet	moreover	for	consequently
so	further	furthermore	then
therefore	thus	accordingly	

Practice 3

Combine the following sentences with words that link equal ideas. Use the words in the list above.

1. I'll practice every night. I'll be ready to perform by next weekend.
2. I am buying camping equipment. I can teach my kids about nature.
3. We could go for a walk. We could go swimming.
4. Milo impresses his boss. He is getting a raise.
5. I do not have enough information. I need to learn more.
6. Our old family photographs are yellow and faded. We are hiring someone to restore them.

Words that Link One Sentence Element to Another
These linking words are used in pairs:

either—or

neither—nor

both—and

not only—but also

whether—or

Practice 4

Fill the spaces in the sentences below with words from the list above.

1. _____ Warren _____ Iris can cook; they eat out a lot.
2. The store carries _____ extra large ___ petite sizes.

3. I speak _____ Spanish _____ French.

4. I am _____ taking yoga classes _____ aerobics.

5. I don't know _____ my daughter is having trouble concentrating _____ just bored in her classes.

6. I would say that _____ Frederick _____ Steffen would be an excellent partner for this project.

Practice 5

The following paragraph offers interview preparation advice, but is written in very poor form. Use all that you have learned about commas and semicolons to make this paragraph flow smoothly. Look above at the two lists of words that link ideas. Use any of these that are appropriate.

> You will want to make a good impression. You will have to dress appropriately for interviews. Go prepared. Learn about the company. Think about your answers to common interview questions. Be clear about your assets and what you have to offer the company. Be prepared to ask questions. Be courteous. Be friendly. Act in a professional manner.

_____

_____

_____

_____

_____

Practice 6

The following paragraph continues to offer good advice in poor form. Continue to link ideas by using words that bring thoughts together.

> Your resume should be neat. It should be clean without errors. The format should be clear. Make your experience and skills easy to find. You may be applying in different fields. If you do this, use different versions of your resume. Make slight changes that emphasize the background and skills that are important for each job. Have someone else read your resume before the interview. Someone else might find errors you missed. Correcting those before the interview will help your chances of getting the job.

_____

_____

_____

_____

_____

Practice 7

Read another choppy paragraph. Then improve it by combining sentences. Use transition or combining words and correct punctuation.

The references you choose to give prospective employers can make the difference. Let people know that you are using them as references. No one should be caught off guard. They may even give some thought to what they would say before the call comes. You don't have to tell people each time you use their names. Just tell them once that you'd like to use them as references and ask if it's okay. References might never be called. It is a good idea to have them lined up and ready for calls just in case.

_____

_____

_____

_____

_____

_____

Building Paragraphs

When you write anything, a report, a letter, or e-mail, for example, you are building paragraphs. Most of the time, you begin with a topic sentence. You want your reader to know as quickly as possible what to expect.

Read the following paragraph. Start by asking yourself, "What is this paragraph about?" Where is the answer to that question? That is the topic sentence. Remember what you learned and practiced about main ideas in the reading section of this book. Main ideas are found in topic sentences.

Example:
Helen Keller—a girl who was deaf and blind—has been a symbol of inspiration for many. She was born in a small farm town in Alabama in 1880 and lost her vision and hearing when she was just 1 year old. When she was 7, her parents hired a tutor to help her. The tutor taught her to use sign language and read Braille; most importantly, she taught her to persevere and have hope. Helen learned from her tutor, Anne Sullivan, how to function in the world, even with her great challenges. Ultimately, Helen went to college and wrote nearly a dozen books. She and Anne toured the world, giving lectures, advice, and inspiration.

You would probably agree that you knew the topic of the paragraph as soon as you read the first sentence. You expected the sentences that followed to tell how Helen Keller's experience was inspirational. The details of those following sentences are supporting details. Again, this brings us back to the concepts you worked with in the beginning of the reading section.

Sometimes writers want to summarize the main idea in the last sentence. They can do that by placing the topic sentence at the end of the paragraph. Consider the following rewrite of the above example.

Example (main idea at the end of a paragraph):
Helen Keller was born in a small farm town in Alabama in 1880 and lost her vision and hearing when she was just 1 year old. When she was 7, her

parents hired a tutor to help her. The tutor taught her to use sign language and read Braille; most importantly, she taught her to persevere and have hope. Helen learned from her tutor, Anne Sullivan, how to function in the world, even with her great challenges. Ultimately, Helen went to college and wrote nearly a dozen books. She and Anne toured the world, giving lectures, advice, and inspiration. Helen Keller—a girl who was deaf and blind—has been, and continues to be, a symbol of inspiration for many.

Practice 8

Read these paragraphs. Find the topic sentence in each one and underline it. List at least two details that support the topic sentence.

Paragraph A

Stanley Kunitz, in his 101 years on Earth, contributed greatly to American poetry. His poetry was published over a period of 75 years. His first book, *Intellectual Things,* was published in 1930 and his last book, *A Poet Reflects on a Century in the Garden,* marked his 100th birthday. He won numerous prizes, including the Pulitzer Prize for Poetry and was appointed twice as the United States poet laureate (a position of great honor for poets). Kunitz was also a teacher, a mentor, and founder of programs to teach aspiring poets and help artists grow, create, connect with other poets, and find avenues for publication.

_____

_____

_____

_____

_____

Paragraph B

Halley's Comet, a poem by Stanley Kunitz, talks about his feelings as a young boy when he learned of the comet in school, a night he sat on the roof waiting for the world to end. He describes the teacher, writing the name of the comet on the blackboard, explaining that if it veered off course, it would be the end of the world. He recalled a wild-eyed preacher by the playground, shouting about the world coming to its end. Supper that night, he recalled, he thought would be his last meal, but he was too excited to eat. At night, he climbed to the roof, a little boy in white flannel, "searching the starry sky, waiting for the world to end."

_____

_____

_____

_____

_____

Practice 9

Notice the logical organization of thoughts in the clearly written paragraph examples. Consider all you have learned about transitions. Follow the directions for each of the following paragraphs. Compare your answers to those in the Answer Key on page 146. (Your answers may be different, yet still correct.)

1. Read the next paragraph. Then insert the following sentence where it belongs: *Some people, however, collect more than a few items of interest.*

   Many people enjoy collecting items they like in small amounts. Almost anything can be searched for by collectors. From stamps, to art glass, to porcelain figures, to old magazines, what is junk to you may be a treasure to someone else. Some people collect so much, they hardly have room to move in their homes.

2. Read the next paragraph. Then insert the following sentence where it belongs: *Some people say the word comes from its original description as a general purpose vehicle, from the slurred sound of the initials GP.*

   The word *jeep* has many possible origins. In fact, a number of theories exist. Others say it was named after a 1930s Popeye character, "Eugene the Jeep," who could go anywhere, even walk the walls and ceilings. Like many unusual words, there will always be some debate over history and origins.

3. Read the next paragraph. Then insert the following sentence where it belongs: *For example, words ending in "um" end in "a" in their plural forms, such as: medium turning to media.*

   The English language is taken from many other languages. In fact, this accounts for a number of irregular words and spellings. Many plurals are irregular. One form of irregular plurals comes from words taken from Greek origins. Another example is the change of *is* to *es*, as in *crisis* to *crises* and *hypothesis* to *hypotheses*. Learning word origins, for many reasons, helps to improve spelling and understand language.

Move the Ideas Along

Transition words fall into a number of different categories, each organizing thoughts in a different way.

Category	Transition Words
Time	now, later, after, before, last, first, while, then, first, second, finally, meanwhile, formerly
Addition	moreover, in addition, besides, too, also, furthermore
Similarity	just as, similarly, in the same way, likewise
Contrast	yet, but, however, although, nevertheless, on the contrary, on the other hand, whereas, nonetheless, in contrast
Illustration	for example, for instance, to illustrate, specifically, in this way
Emphasis	indeed, clearly, in fact, certainly
Conclusion	therefore, consequently, in conclusion, in other words

Example: First, I want to thank my team for their hard work. Secondly, I want to thank our parent company for the equipment and support that allows us to do our best work. Last, and certainly not least, I thank my family for their patience through all these months of my working late and through the weekends.

Practice 10

Paragraph 1

Fill in the blanks with the correct time-based transitions.

To install this computer application, _____ quit all open programs. _____, insert the installation disk and select "install." _____, stay by the computer to follow any commands during installation. _____, restart the computer and open the application to see that it is working. You should see a tutorial option as soon as you open the program.

Paragraph 2

Use two of these connecting words (contrast words) to build your paragraph: *however, on the other hand, likewise,* or *nevertheless.*

Many adopted children search for their birth parents. Many birth parents search for their children, hoping to find they have had happy lives. Agencies will not give parents' information if they do not know that the parents want to be found. The Internet is a tool used often to find people's backgrounds and contact information, assisting many with searches.

Answer Key: Section 3, Lesson 6

Practice 1

There is more than one possible answer for some; the key is to ensure that all sentence elements are parallel. Review each answer carefully to see the parallel structures.

1. My new suit is simple, stylish, and professional.
2. I worked late every night this week because two people in the department were sick.
3. We both like to walk on the beach and ride on the bike path.
4. The book was clear, informative, and well written.
5. My favorite team sports are football, softball, and volleyball.
6. Henry is not only a good friend, but also a great boss.
7. My doctor gives me advice on relaxation, nutrition, and exercise.
8. Ron plays guitar, Rocky sings, and I play the drums.
9. The supervisor wrote the incident report clearly, promptly, and fairly.
10. Julianne is fair and honest.
11. Meditation is both relaxing and peaceful.

Practice 2

Possible answers:

1. The film festival will be running all week; therefore, I don't care if we miss the opening night.

    Or

    Because the film festival will be running all week, I don't care if we miss the opening night.
2. I got a new cell phone plan because I found one that offers more minutes.
3. I sent in the nomination, though it's late and may not be considered.
4. I called for service this morning, though no one has called back yet.
5. I won't use that color if you don't like it.
6. Because my boss screams all the time, I am looking for a new job.
7. I want to work at the clinic where I can help people.
8. This tea tastes terrible because the water here isn't clean.

Practice 3

More than one answer is possible for most; at least one correct answer is provided for each.

1. I'll practice every night; then, I'll be ready to perform by next weekend.
2. I am buying camping equipment so I can teach my kids about nature.
3. We could go for a walk and a swim.
4. Milo impresses his boss; consequently, he is getting a raise.
5. I do not have enough information, thus I need to learn more.
6. Our old family photographs are yellow and faded, so we are hiring someone to restore them.

Practice 4

1. Neither, nor
2. both, and; *or* not only, but also; *or* neither, nor
3. both, and; *or* not only, but also; *or* neither, nor
4. not only, but also; *or* both, and; *or* neither, nor
5. whether, or
6. either, or; *or* neither, nor

Practice 5

Suggested correction:

Because you will want to make a good impression, dress appropriately for interviews. Go prepared: learn about the company and think about your answers to common interview questions. Additionally, be clear about your assets and what you have to offer the company and be prepared to ask questions. Finally, be courteous, friendly, and professional.

Practice 6

Suggested correction:

Your resume should be neat, clean and correct. The format should be clear, with your experience and skills easy to find. You may be applying in different fields, and, if you do, use different versions of your resume. Make slight changes that emphasize the background and skills that are important for each job. Have someone else, who might find errors you missed, read your resume before the interview. Correcting those before the interview will help your chances of getting the job.

Practice 7

Suggested correction:

The references you choose to give prospective employers can make the difference. Let people know that you are using them as references because no one should be caught off guard; they may even give some thought to what they would say before the call comes. You don't have to tell people each time you use their names; however, tell them once that you'd like to use them as references and ask if it's okay. Although references might never be called, it is a good idea to have them lined up and ready for calls just in case.

Practice 8

Paragraph A

Main Idea: *You should have underlined the first sentence.*

Supporting Details:

- His poetry was published over a period of 75 years
- won numerous prizes, including the Pulitzer Prize for Poetry
- was appointed twice as the United States poet laureate
- was a teacher and a mentor
- founded programs for poets

Paragraph B

Main Idea: *You should have underlined the first sentence.*

- describes the teacher, saying it could be the end of the world
- recalled a preacher shouting about the end of the world
- says he thought his dinner would be his last meal

- was excited
- climbed to the roof "searching the starry sky, waiting for the world to end"

Practice 9

1. Many people enjoy collecting items they like in small amounts. *Some people, however, collect more than a few items of interest.* Almost anything can be searched for by collectors. From stamps, to art glass, to porcelain figures to old magazines, what is junk to you may be a treasure to someone else. Some people collect so much they hardly have room to move in their homes.

2. The word *jeep* has many possible origins. In fact, a number of theories exist. *Some people say the word comes from its original description as a general purpose vehicle, from the slurred sound of the initials GP.* Others say it was named after a 1930s Popeye character, "Eugene the Jeep," who could go anywhere, even walk the walls and ceilings. Like many unusual words, there will always be some debate over history and origins.

3. The English language is taken from many other languages. In fact, this accounts for a number of irregular words and spellings. Many plurals are irregular. One form of irregular plurals comes from words taken from Greek origins. *For example, words ending in "um" end in "a" in their plural forms, such as: medium turning to media.* Another example is the change of *is* to *es,* as in *crisis* to *crises* and *hypothesis* to *hypotheses.* Learning word origins, for many reasons, helps to improve spelling and understand language.

Practice 10

Paragraph 1

To install this computer application, *first* quit all open programs. *Then,* insert the installation disk and select "install." *Meanwhile,* stay by the computer to follow any commands during installation. *Finally,* restart the computer and open the application to see that it is working. You should see a tutorial option as soon as you open the program.

Paragraph 2

Many adopted children search for their birth parents. *Likewise,* many birth parents search for their children, hoping to find they have had happy lives. *Nevertheless,* agencies will not give parents' information if they do not know that the parents want to be found. *However,* the Internet is a tool used often to find people's backgrounds and contact information, assisting many with searches.

Language Posttest

For questions 1–3, decide which punctuation mark, if any, is needed in the sentence:

1. I have been studying hard and I need a break!

   A   ;

   B   :

   C   ,

   D   None

2. The movie was, in fact based on a true story.

   A   ;

   B   :

   C   ,

   D   None

3. George had been working for the company for three years before he was promoted.

   A   ,

   B   "

   C   ;

   D   None

For questions 4–6, choose the word or phrase that best completes the sentence.

4. Keeping up with bills _____ more difficult since the last rent increase.

   A   became

   B   has become

   C   is becoming

   D   has been becoming

5. Among the three partners, Antoine's investment is the _____.

   A   larger

   B   large

   C   largest

   D   most large

6. Charlene is going to start _____ a dance class every Tuesday night.

   A   takes

   B   taking

   C   is taking

   D   took

For questions 7–17, choose the sentence that is written correctly and shows the correct capitalization and punctuation. Be sure the sentence you choose is complete.

7.
A I am upgrading my website.
B Adding a blog.
C Hired a web Designer to help me.
D My new colors black white and gold.

8.
A Hurricane warnings along the coast.
B My wallet was stolen, my credit cards, cash, and driver's license.
C The tour guide showed us the best restaurants in the city, most were very expensive.
D My family and I will be spending two weeks in Phoenix, Arizona.

9.
A Of the two of us, I am the better driver.
B Among the eight of us, Ned is the more talented.
C Between the two of us I am the oldest.
D Of the films two directors Hans is a perfectionist.

10.
A I don't know why the printer keeps breaking down?
B Can't you take a later lunch break.
C Did the letter ask for an "itemized list?"
D I thought she said, "Send the package by Monday."

11.
A My favorite course, "The History of Nature", is taught by Maria Roberts.
B Last year I had a course called "The Nature of History."
C The article, "Fear of Eggs," was about salmonella poisoning.
D The camera's digital zoom lens, took detailed photographs, of even the smallest insects.

12.
A My new computer, an Apple has more features than my old PC.
B In a neighborhood of gardeners, my mother grows the biggest tomatoes.
C I love fruit; but only buy organic.
D I buy organic, because I worry about the dangers of pesticides in food.

13.
A I didn't hardly think Daniel would finish school.
B My neighbor Vera ain't no gourmet cook.
C It isn't no surprise that Travis won an award for his hard work.
D Paul's wife, Andrea, is an interior decorator.

14.

  A Steam was raising from the hot coffee.

  B Antoine was raising up his son well.

  C Remmi was raised good.

  D Bart is raising his sons to respect women.

15.

  A Were going to buy new shoes.

  B Children outgrow clothe's very quickly.

  C Ted's dogs were waiting anxiously to go out.

  D My old socks' haven't any wholes in them.

16.

  A The new playground equipment are made mostly of recycled tires.

  B Sports, on television, is less exciting than the feeling of being at the game.

  C The next book on the reading list, *Angela's Ashes,* was written by Frank McCourt.

  D Cape May are a lovely beach town in New Jersey.

17.

  A "The book list," explained the teacher, "is taken from the book titled: *Book Lust.*"

  B "This is a long list" exclaimed Ray!

  C An author came to speak to the class and they "quoted him" in their papers.

  D The instructor asked, "Do you have any questions"?

For questions 18–21, read the underlined sentences. Then choose the sentence that best combines those sentences into one.

18. My boss gave me a raise.
I have brought in more new accounts than anyone else in the company.

   A   If my boss gave me a raise, I have brought in more new accounts than anyone else in the company.

   B   My boss gave me a raise, but I have brought in more new accounts than anyone else in the company.

   C   I have brought in more new accounts than anyone else in the company, but my boss gave me a raise.

   D   Because I have brought in more new accounts than anyone else in the company, my boss gave me a raise.

19. The company is laying people off.
Company profits are falling.

   A   The company is laying people off and, as a result, profits are falling.

   B   Because profits are falling, the company is laying people off.

   C   Since the company is laying people off, profits are falling.

   D   Company profits are falling, but the company is laying people off.

20. The photographer added a rich glow to the golden leaves of her autumn photographs.
The photographer used computer software to add the glow.

   A   The photographer used computer software to add a rich glow to the golden leaves of her autumn photographs.

   B   The photographer added a rich glow to the golden leaves of her autumn photographs; nevertheless, she used computer software.

   C   Because the photographer added a rich glow to the golden leaves of her autumn photographs, she used computer software.

   D   Adding a rich glow to the golden leaves of her autumn photographs, the photographer then used computer software to add the glow.

21. The writer used humor to make a serious point.
She used humor beautifully.

   A   The beautiful writer used humor to make a serious point.

   B   The writer used humor to make a serious point beautiful.

   C   The writer used humor beautifully to make a serious point.

   D   The writer, using humor, makes a serious point beautiful.

For questions 22–27, read the paragraph. Then choose the sentence that best fills the blank in the paragraph.

22. _____. A resume that is wrinkled gives an immediate bad impression. Typos and spelling errors give the impression of someone who is careless. An interviewer sees resumes like this as indicators of people who don't take pride in themselves or their work. It's always a good idea to have someone else read your resume to look for errors you might have missed.

A What is most important, in resume writing, is just to get something down on paper.

B Employers look not only at the content of a resume, but the condition.

C Use subheadings in your resume.

D Do not wear wrinkled clothes to an interview.

23. _____. However, the hardship does tend to bring families and neighborhoods closer together. Neighborhoods gather to share food and keep company. Without televisions, computers, or even bustling offices to get to, we get to know each other. Children play outside. And, sitting outside at night, realizing how lucky we are to have each other, we look up and see the stars in a way this city hasn't seen them since the last blackout.

A Loss of electricity after a hurricane has some positive effects.

B Loss of electricity after a hurricane leaves residents and businesses struggling as power crews slowly restore our lives to "normal."

C The power company works hard after a hurricane.

D Hurricanes can be fun.

24. Prescription drugs often have a long list of side effects. Drugs also react with one another, so it is very important to have one doctor who knows all of the drugs you are taking. Medicine should not be taken lightly and it can be dangerous to take someone else's prescribed medicine. _____.

   A   Therefore, many natural alternative treatments work well without side effects.

   B   In conclusion, many natural alternative treatments work well without side effects.

   C   Similarly, many natural alternative treatments work well without side effects.

   D   On the other hand, many natural alternative treatments work well without side effects.

25. Blogs are a popular outlet for writing. Blogs may be used as online diaries or to post articles, news, or commentary. Readers can bookmark a blog or subscribe so they can see when a new entry has been posted. The term "blog" came from combining the words, "web log." _____

   A   People who write blogs are known as "bloggers."

   B   Therefore, people who write blogs are known as "bloggers."

   C   However, people who write blogs are known as "bloggers."

   D   People who are known as "bloggers" are a trusted source of information.

26. In Victorian times, flowers held special meanings and those who received a certain flower in a particular color knew exactly what message it carried. For instance, a small white bell flower showed gratitude while a white clover said, "think of me," and Iceland moss wished good health. The rose, an ancient symbol of love and beauty, still holds several meanings, and some people still know that white is for purity and pink for grace. _____.

   A   There are more than one hundred species of wild roses.

   B   Though most flowers have lost their Victorian meanings, a red rose will always symbolize romantic love.

   C   A white wedding gown is also a symbol of purity.

   D   If you sleep next to Iceland moss you will not get sick.

27. _____. As a result, chemical-free products and natural alternatives are becoming more popular. These products are available in health food stores and many are slowly becoming available in major chains. Natural products are also available online, through catalogues. Many have such simple ingredient lists that they are easy to make yourself and a number of books offer instructions on how to make your own natural products.

A   Natural products are becoming more popular.

B   You, too, can make your own natural products at home in a few easy steps!

C   More and more people are developing allergies to chemicals.

D   Health food stores carry a wide variety of natural products.

For questions 28 and 29, choose the answer that best develops the topic sentence.

28. Technology was supposed to make our lives easier.

   A   Nothing important was really invented in the last five years.

   B   Nothing of value comes easily.

   C   The fast pace of technology has, instead, increased expectations rather than giving us more free time.

   D   The fast pace of technology has also increased expectations rather than giving us more free time.

29. Good, clear writing is a skill that anyone can develop.

   A   Tom Clancy is a famous writer.

   B   Many writers enjoy the feel of a good fountain pen.

   C   Like any skill, it takes study, practice, and patience.

   D   Journal writing is a good way to explore your feelings.

For questions 30 and 31, read the paragraph. Then choose the sentence that does not *belong in the paragraph.*

30. (1) Some children's books and films are so well done that adults enjoy them, as well. (2) *The Little Prince* is a book for children that is loved and often quoted by adults. Many Disney films attract adults, even without children. (3) Fairy tales and fables are especially loved by children. (4) A well-told story can cross the boundaries of age, making adults feel like children and reminding us of the simple truths we sometimes forget in the business of daily life.

31. (1) Photography has changed dramatically over the years. (2) Digital point-and-shoot cameras have simplified what was once a complex process. (3) Effects that used to take a long time to learn can now be achieved by using very simple computer software. (4) Certain websites allow subscribers to purchase digital photographs online.

For questions 32–54, read the passage and the letter and look at the numbered, underlined parts. Choose the answer that is written correctly for each underlined part.

When looking for a job, consider what is important to you. Salary is always a strong motivator, but (32) other motivators include perks benefits and work atmosphere. If you love adventure, travel benefits may mean (33) more than a biggest check. A job that offers a lower salary but great health insurance may be important to you. You have a lot to consider and, if you have a family, you have to think of (34) they're necessities, too. Your earnings are more than your salary. When deciding whether a job meets your salary requirements, (35) they should remember to calculate all financial and lifestyle benefits.

32.

  A other motivators include perks, benefits, and work atmosphere

  B other motivators include, perks; benefits; and work atmosphere

  C other motivators include, perks benefits and work atmosphere

  D other motivators include; perks, benefits, and work atmosphere

33.

  A more than a most biggest check

  B more than a big check

  C more than a more bigger check

  D Correct as is

34.

  A their necessities

  B they are necessities

  C there necessities

  D Correct as is

35.

  A remembering

  B have been remembering

  C have to remember

  D you should remember

Sunnyside Daycare Centers

76 Trumble Avenue

Seattle, Washington 98101

(36) march 21, 2008

(37) Dear Mr. Grasso

It was a pleasure to meet you at the job fair (38) last week I am sending my resume, as we discussed. I hope to hear from you to discuss possible career options at (39) Sunnyside daycare centers. You can reach (40) myself at 318-444-0822. Thank you for (41) you're consideration.

(42) Sincerely

Ronald Bell

36.

    A   March 21 2008

    B   March, 21, 2008

    C   March 21, 2008

    D   march 21. 2008

37.

    A   Dear Mr. Grasso—

    B   Dear Mr. Grasso:

    C   Dear Mr. Grasso...

    D   Dear mr. Grasso:

38.

    A   last week, I am sending

    B   last week. I am sending

    C   last week, but I am sending

    D   last week; however, I am sending

39.

    A   sunnyside daycare centers

    B   Sunnyside Daycare Centers

    C   The Sunnyside daycare centers

    D   Correct as is

40.

    A   me, myself

    B   my self

    C   me

    D   Me

41.

    A   your

    B   you are

    C   yore

    D   yourself

42.

    A   Sincerely:

    B   Sincerely;

    C   Sincerely,

    D   Sincerely.

Humphrey Bogart and Lauren Bacall had one of the greatest on-screen romances of all time. They delivered their (43) quick fun dialogue perfectly. (44) Most of all, the chemistry between them was undeniable. The actors first met while filming (45) *To Have And Have Not*. They married and had two (46) children. Stephen and Leslie.

43.

   A   quick; fun dialogue

   B   quickly fun dialogue

   C   quick, fun dialogue

   D   quick, however fun dialogue

44.

   A   However,

   B   In spite of that,

   C   In contrast,

   D   Correct as is

45.

   A   *To have and have not*

   B   *To Have and Have Not*

   C   *To Have and Have not*

   D   *To Have; and Have Not*

46.

   A   children; Stephen and Leslie.

   B   Children, Stephen and Leslie.

   C   children and Stephen and Leslie.

   D   children, Stephen and Leslie.

(47) Jims family works with him. He started a business from home and everyone in the family pitches in. His wife acts as his public relations department and their children help in small ways (48) such as taking messages and make address labels. (49) His kids say It's fun to see the things we do used in business. (50) The clients are terrible nice." Of course, Jim doesn't push them to work too many hours; he wants them to concentrate on school and play.

47.

   A   Jim's

   B   Jim's is

   C   Jims'

   D   Jim is

48.

   A   such taking messages and making address labels

   B   such as took messages and made address labels

   C   such as taking messages and making address labels

   D   such as take messages and make address labels

49.

A His kids say, "It's fun to see

B His kids says, "It's fun to see

C His kid say, "It's fun to see

D His kids say "Its fun to see

50.

A The clients are terrible nicely."

B The clients are terribly nice".

C The clients' are terribly nice.

D The clients are terribly nice."

Because of his training, Bob (51) is efficienter than Millie. Millie is smart and (52) can learn fast but she needs more training. Her supervisors say she is an asset and are recommending that the company pay for her to attend courses. She is excited about the opportunity and Bob (53) has offering to help (54) hers with her studies.

51.

A is efficient

B is more efficient

C is most efficient

D is more efficienter

52.

A can learn fast; but

B learns fast, but

C can learn fast; but though

D learns fast and though

53.

A has offers

B has offered

C has offering

D offering

54.

A her's

B hers'

C her

D Correct as is

Answer Key: Section 3, Lesson 6 (Posttest)

1. C	**2.** C	**3.** D	**4.** B	**5.** C	**6.** B
7. A	**8.** D	**9.** A	**10.** D	**11.** C	**12.** B
13. D	**14.** D	**15.** C	**16.** C	**17.** A	**18.** D
19. B	**20.** A	**21.** C	**22.** B	**23.** B	**24.** D
25. A	**26.** B	**27.** C	**28.** C	**29.** C	**30.** 3
31. 4	**32.** A	**33.** B	**34.** A	**35.** D	**36.** C
37. B	**38.** B	**39.** B	**40.** C	**41.** A	**42.** C
43. C	**44.** D	**45.** B	**46.** D	**47.** A	**48.** C
49. A	**50.** D	**51.** B	**52.** B	**53.** B	**54.** C

To ensure that you have mastered the skills in the Language Section:

1. Once you have checked your answers against the answer key, go back to compare your incorrect answers with the correct ones. Notice whether you understand why the answer given is the correct one.

2. Total your number of correct answers out of the 54 possible answers. If you had **fewer than 49 correct answers**, find the sections that explain your incorrect answers and review them carefully. If you had **fewer than 45 correct answers**, take some extra time to go back through the Language Section. Look at each incorrect answer throughout the section and go back to the corresponding lesson to see that you understand why each answer given is the correct one.

3. Before taking the TABE test, come back to review the Language Section. Pay special attention to areas that were difficult or confusing, but scan the entire section again to make sure that you feel confident in knowing and using these skills.

LESSON 1 The ABC's of Learning to Spell

Studying the spelling of a particular word is useful; spell, say, and practice new words. Keeping a diary of new words is a good way to both improve your spelling and increase your vocabulary. However, you cannot learn every word you need to learn one by one. This is why learning the rules and exceptions is more useful than simply trying to learn by memorizing the spelling of each word. Take your time learning the rules before you go to the posttest. In addition, review the "Commonly Misspelled Words" listed after the posttest. Think, as you look through the list, of how the spelling of troublesome words fits into a rule you learned.

STUDY TIPS

1 Learn the rules.
2 Keep a notebook handy to record and learn new words.
3 Break the word down into syllables and say it out loud. It might help if you close your eyes and picture the word.
4 Apply the rules you learn to new words as you come across them.

Stay with new words until they are yours. Go back in a few days to words you think you know to ensure that you do.

Spelling Pretest

For questions 1–20, choose the word that is spelled correctly and best completes the sentence.

1. The singer was _____ when her voice cracked.

   A embarassed

   B embarrased

   C embarased

   D embarrassed

2. The meeting was called to _____ all of our good work.

   A acknoledge

   B acknowledge

   C aknowledge

   D acknowlege

3. The drinks were _____.

   A complimentary

   B complementary

   C complamentery

   D complamenary

4. The clerk put the _____ in the bag.

   A recete

   B reciept

   C receipt

   D receit

5. Please fill out the enclosed _____.

   A questionnaire

   B questionaire

   C questionnare

   D questionare

6. If I am offered the job, I plan to send an _____ letter.

   A acceptince

   B acceptance

   C acceptunce

   D acceptonce

7. I am going to school to become a computer _____.

   A programmer

   B programmar

   C programur

   D programar

8. The _____ shows the company's chain of command.

   A diagram

   B diegram

   C diugram

   D daigram

9. I read labels for the _____ count.

   A calory

   B calore

   C calorie

   D callorie

10. I don't like any of the candidates running for the _____.

   A presidentcy

   B presidentsy

   C presidency

   D presidancy

11. I went to the pharmacy to get my
_____ filled.

   A   perscription

   B   purscription

   C   prescription

   D   proscription

12. Our dinner reservation is at the new
Italian _____ downtown.

   A   restarant

   B   restourant

   C   restrant

   D   restaurant

13. The two cousins always had a warm
_____.

   A   relationship

   B   relasionship

   C   relachionship

   D   relacionship

14. When you request an interview, the
human resource department will
answer your _____.

   A   querry

   B   query

   C   querie

   D   querry

15. Chemical pollution is hurting the
_____.

   A   enviornment

   B   enviernment

   C   environment

   D   environmint

16. _____ is my day off.

   A   Wendsday

   B   Wenesday

   C   Wensday

   D   Wednesday

17. The computer comes with a service
_____.

   A   guarantee

   B   guarentee

   C   guaranty

   D   garenty

18. The couple took _____ vows.

   A   there

   B   their

   C   they're

   D   there's

19. The flight was delayed because of the
plane's broken electrical _____.

   A   sistem

   B   systam

   C   system

   D   sistam

20. Nadia runs two _____.

   A   busines

   B   busnisses

   C   businesses

   D   bussiness

Answer Key: Section 4, Lesson 1 (Pretest)

Check your answers with the ones in this chart. Total the number of your correct responses at the bottom of the answer key. Then read the recommendations that follow.

1. D	**2.** B	**3.** A	**4.** C	**5.** A
6. B	**7.** A	**8.** A	**9.** C	**10.** C
11. C	**12.** D	**13.** A	**14.** B	**15.** C
16. D	**17.** A	**18.** B	**19.** C	**20.** C

To discover your areas for skill improvement in the Spelling Section:

1. Once you have checked your answers against the answer key, go back to compare your incorrect answers with the correct ones. Rewrite those words with their correct spellings on a separate sheet of paper and go back to review them.

2. Total your number of correct answers out of the 20 possible answers. If you had 17 or more correct, you did very well. However, spelling rules and exceptions are especially tricky, so pay special attention to this section even if you scored well.

3. Keep the sheet of paper with the words you misspelled on the pretest and review it once you have completed the chapter. For each word, consider whether you have learned a rule that will help you spell similar words in the future and on the TABE test.

Spelling Basics

1. Vowels: *a, e, i, o, u,* and sometimes *y*

   A Vowel sounds can be short, as in the *a* in *attitude* or the *e* in *rest.*

   B Vowels sounds can be long, as in the *i* in *line* or the *o* in *role.*

   C The vowel *y* provides a different sound depending on the word in which it is used: *lazy* (long *e*), *rhythmic* (short *i*).

   D Vowel sounds are sometimes dropped, or not clearly long or short. Listen to the *o* in *conclude* or the first *e* in *absence.* They are dropped vowel sounds, meaning it's hard to tell by ear which vowel is being used. A dropped vowel sound is called a *schwa.* In the dictionary, the schwa is printed this way: ∂

2. Consonants: the rest of the alphabet

   A Very different letters often have the same sound, such as the *j* in *jaw* and the *dg* in *edge.*

   B Combinations of consonants and vowels also often sound the same but are spelled differently, for example, as in the *tia, cia,* and *cea* of *partial, crucial,* and *ocean.*

   C Many letters are silent; consider the *gh* in *right* or *night.*

   D Many words sound the same but have different meanings, such as *whether* (as in "whether or not") and *weather* (temperature, etc.), *right* and *write, through* and *threw, break* and *brake, meet* and *meat.* These are called *homonyms.*

   E Other words are spelled alike, though they have different meanings, as in *rose* (flower) and *rose* (stood up), and there are countless examples of these. Just open your dictionary to find how many definitions are listed for typical words. Look up the word *run* to give you an idea of just how many meanings one word can have.

   F Some words are spelled the same and have different pronunciations. Consider the accent shift from *invalid* (not valid) to *invalid* (handicapped person).

   G Syllables are units of sound that make up a word. Any word that contains more than one syllable has an accent mark on one of those syllables.

Example: bi-OG′-ra-phy. This word is made up of four syllables. Say it out loud. Can you hear the accent or stress in the second syllable?

Practice 1

Say each of these words and put an accent mark over the syllable you stress.

1. tomorrow
2. writer
3. together

4. festive

5. trustworthy

6. technical

7. considerate

8. normal

9. indecent

10. dictionary

Prefix and Suffix Rules

The first rules you will review and practice are prefix and suffix rules. A *prefix* is added to the front of a word and a *suffix* is added to the end. These alter meaning, and spelling is sometimes changed when they are added.

Prefix Rule: Prefixes do not change the spelling of a word.

Prefix	Meaning	Root Word	New Word
ir-	not	regular	irregular
un-	not	necessary	unnecessary
mal-	badly	nourished	malnourished
re-	again	recorded	rerecorded
bi-	two	cycle	bicycle

Notice the two *n*'s in *unnecessary* and the two *r*'s in *irregular*. Usually, neither the prefix nor the word changes, even if a letter is repeated.

Examples: misspell, irrational, cooperate

Special Cases: When *all* is used as a prefix, the second *l* is dropped.

all + ways = always
all + together = altogether

Practice 2

Add the following prefixes to the words below.

ir-, ill-, il-, im-, un-

1. possible

2. legal

3. responsible

4. important

5. moral

6. advised

7. relevant

8. moved

9. conceived

10. rational

Suffix Rules

1. **Suffix that begins with a consonant: spelling does not change (with a few exceptions)**

careless	-ness	carelessness
help	-ful	helpful
stubborn	-ness	stubbornness
love	-ly	lovely
hand	-fuls	handfuls

   Exceptions: *truly, duly, education*

2. **Word ends in *e* + a suffix that begins with a consonant: *do not* drop the *e***

hope	-ful	hopeful
excite	-ment	excitement
love	-ly	lovely
grace	-ful	graceful

3. **Word ends in *e* + a suffix that begins with a vowel: *do* drop the *e***

continue	-al	continual
large	-est	largest
imagine	-ary	imaginary
engage	-ing	engaging

   Exceptions: Words that end in *ge* or *ce* keep the final *e* when adding the suffixes *able* or *ous* (in order to retain the soft sound of *g* or *e*): *courageous, manageable, noticeable, outrageous, peaceable, serviceable, traceable, noticeable, changeable*

4. **Words that end in *y*: most suffixes change the spelling of that word**

happy	-ness	happiness
lazy	-est	laziest
sorry	-er	sorrier
study	-ed	studied

   Exceptions: If the *y* is preceded by a vowel or the ending is *ing*, the spelling does not change: *payment, studying, playing, prayer*

   (It's easy to remember that the *y* doesn't change when adding *ing* because common English words do not have two *i*'s in a row—as in *studiing*, or *priing*. Of course, the word *skiing* has two *i*'s, but the original word, *ski*, ends in an *i*.)

   More exceptions to remember: *dry* and *dryness, shy* and *shyly* or *shyness*

Practice 3

Circle the incorrectly spelled word in each sentence and write the correct spelling beside the sentence.

1. My daughter has imagineary friends and she talks to them, noticeably, in class.

2. It is not true that people with the largest bank accounts are happyest.

3. You look truley lovely in that outfit.

4. My friend accidently turned her hair blue when she was dyeing it.

5. My aunt, who has a strong educational background, has been helpfull to me in finding the right school.

6. My mind is not changable on this and I would be happier if we did not discuss it.

7. I could not be sorryer that my laziness cost us this client.

8. I am not comfterble with this line of questioning.

9. I usually wear hiking boots in the desert because I am afraid of poisonnous snakes.

10. I am working and studying overtime to qualify for the managment training program.

Suffix Rules Continued

5. **Most one-syllable words (when the last three letters are consonant + vowel + consonant): double the final consonant when adding a suffix that begins with a vowel.**

rot	-en	rotten
plan	-ed	planned
top	-ing	topping
crab	-by	crabby
blog	-er	blogger

Exceptions: Words ending in *c,* add *k* before a suffix beginning with *e, i,* or *y*: *picnic* becomes *picnicked, panic* becomes *panicky.*

Notice that double vowels preceding a final consonant do not follow this rule: *bookish, cooking, seeker, woolen*

6. **Most two-syllable words (when the last three letters are consonant + vowel + consonant): double final consonant before changing word form *only when* the accent is on the last syllable.**

rewrap	-ed	rewrapped
occur	-ence	occurrence
refer	-al	referral
defer	-ed	deferred

Careful! Remember that this rule does not apply when the accent is on the first syllable.

Examples of first syllable accents: *rivet—riveted, summon—summoned, planet—planetary, rival—rivalry, baker—bakery*

Exceptions: As always, there are exceptions: *renew* becomes *renewed* (Some consonants, such as *w*, are never repeated when adding a suffix.)

Practice 4

Circle the incorrectly spelled word in each sentence.

1. Andre is finally running for city government. He has planed to for years now.
2. Laura has been shy and bookish, but she is a strong reader and far ahead in her studys. She is just now beginning to get comfortable socially.
3. Tony is raceing Tanya this Sunday. I'm betting on Tanya, but Harold says Tony will be the winner.
4. Our party planner charged us for changeing the date at the last minute.
5. The reporter forgot his questions in the excitment and started acting like all the other fans.
6. Everything went wrong with the party planning, right down to the rotten cake topping. But it was a beautiful stary night and we were all good friends, so the party was still successful.
7. It occurred to me too late that I might be able to get a refund if I had returnned the merchandise within the first week.
8. After the hurricane, I became panicky every time a storm was comming.

Plural Word Rules

1. **Add an *s* to most words.**

computers	vans
cats	planes
incidents	tests

2. **Add *es* to words ending in *o* or preceded by a consonant.**

heroes	tomatoes
potatoes	echoes
ghettoes	vetoes

   Exceptions: all musical terms ending in *o*, including *pianos, altos, solos, cellos, sopranos*. Other exceptions: *gazebos, casinos*.

3. **Add only an *s* to words that end in a vowel plus *o* (*ao, eo, io, oo, uo*).**

stereo	stereos
studio	studios
duo	duos

4. **Add _es_ to words ending in _s, sh, ch,_ and _x._**

classes	bosses
riches	marshes
sexes	boxes

5. **Change _y_ to _i_ and add _es_ in words that end in _y_ preceded by a consonant.**

fly	try	study	berry
flies	tries	studies	berries

Practice 5

Circle the incorrectly spelled words below. Write the word with its correct spelling beside each sentence.

1. We grow strawberries, tomatos, and herbs.
2. Uri sometimes sings soloes and sometimes sings with his backup singers, both sopranos, and records his music in some well-known studios.
3. My bosses are concerned about the company's loses.
4. The stereos in the store emit strong echos.
5. My brother flies to Las Vegas every year to play in the casinoes.
6. Hanna always looses her lighter, so she keeps boxes of matches in every drawer.

Plural Rules Continued

6. **Words ending in _ful_ form their plurals by adding _s_ to the end of the word.**

mouthfuls	handfuls

7. **A compound word forms its plural by adding _s_ to the main word.**

brothers-in-law   mothers-in-law

8. **Some words keep the same spelling for singular and plural forms.**

deer	sheep
fish	offspring

9. **Some words form their plurals by irregular changes.**

child	children
foot	feet
person	people
tooth	teeth
mouse	mice

10. **Most words that end in *f* or *fe* have plurals that end in *ves*.**

knife	knives
life	lives
wife	wives
self	selves
half	halves
wolf	wolves
loaf	loaves

Exceptions: *beliefs, reefs, chiefs*

More exceptions: Words ending in *ff* do not change form.

puffs, sniffs, cuffs, cliffs

Practice 6

Circle the incorrectly spelled word in each sentence.

1. The children have pet mices.
2. My sisters-in-law live in a town where deers come right into the backyard.
3. The dog's offsprings are up for adoption to any people who will give them a good home.
4. My son-in-laws eat handfuls of candy and their teeth are filled with cavities.
5. I have two loafs of bread and two knives, so let's put one loaf at each end of the table.

Additional Rules

Rule: *i* before *e* except after *c*

relief	believe
chief	niece
field	yield

Exceptions: *e* before *i* in words that have a long *a* sound

neighbor, weigh

More exceptions: *weird, leisure, neither, seize*

Rule: *sede, ceed,* and *cede*

Only three words are spelled with a *ceed* ending:

exceed   proceed   succeed

Only one word is spelled with the *sede* ending:

supersede

Others end in *cede*:

concede   precede   secede

Practice 7

Circle the incorrectly spelled word in each sentence.

1. My neice is dating my neighbor.
2. I will never succeed at getting my finances in order if I continually excede my credit limit.
3. I work in the nutrition feild and have been dieting for years now, but still weigh the same as when I started.
4. I do beleive that herbs offer relief for many common ailments.
5. I am about to consede defeat.

PRACTICE REVIEW

Circle the incorrectly spelled word in each sentence.

1. I have always had a good relashionship with my parents and siblings.
2. My sister is hopeing to be a famous actress.
3. I don't know how to handel this complicated problem.
4. I always loose my keys.
5. I axed the teacher a question regarding US history.
6. The cameras are roleing, but please try to act naturally.
7. I am going to address the board conserning my noisy neighbors.
8. She is the rudist, most discourteous woman I have ever known.
9. Are you ridding home with your coworkers today?
10. The bank has several checking and savings acount options.

Answer Key: Section 4, Lesson 1

Practice 1

1. to**mor**'row
2. **wri**'ter
3. to**geth**'er
4. **fes**'tive
5. **trust**'worthy
6. **tech**'nical
7. con**sid**'erate
8. **nor**'mal
9. in**de**'cent
10. **dic**'tionary

Practice 2

1. impossible
2. illegal

3. irresponsible
4. unimportant
5. immoral
6. illadvised
7. irrelevant
8. unmoved
9. illconceived
10. irrational

Practice 3

1. imaginary
2. happiest
3. truly
4. accidentally
5. helpful
6. changeable
7. sorrier
8. comfortable
9. poisonous
10. management

Practice 4

1. planned
2. studies
3. racing
4. changing
5. excitement
6. starry
7. returned
8. coming

Practice 5

1. tomatoes
2. solos
3. losses
4. echoes
5. casinos
6. loses

Practice 6

1. mice
2. deer
3. offspring
4. sons-in-law
5. loaves

Practice 7

1. niece
2. exceed
3. field
4. believe
5. concede

Spelling Review

1. relationship
2. hoping
3. handle
4. lose
5. asked
6. rolling
7. concerning
8. rudest
9. riding
10. account

Spelling Posttest

For questions 1–20, choose the word that is spelled correctly and best completes the sentence.

1. We plan on voting in the _____ election.

   A   congressionol

   B   congressionnal

   C   congresional

   D   congressional

2. You need a _____ driver's license.

   A   valud

   B   valed

   C   valid

   D   valed

3. Raising a child takes a great deal of _____.

   A   patiense

   B   patience

   C   patiance

   D   pationce

4. I can't paint the outside of the house without _____.

   A   assistence

   B   assistance

   C   asistance

   D   assistanse

5. At _____, we met our friends in the lobby.

   A   intermission

   B   intermision

   C   intermisun

   D   intermissien

6. It certainly wasn't a _____ error.

   A   conscious

   B   consious

   C   conscius

   D   conscios

7. The mask added _____ to the costume.

   A   mystury

   B   mystery

   C   mistery

   D   mysstery

8. I manage all of the _____ in the office.

   A   corespondance

   B   coruspondence

   C   corespondence

   D   correspondence

9. That car has great _____ on icy roads.

   A   stobility

   B   stebility

   C   stubility

   D   stability

10. The museum paid _____ to the artist.

    A   homaje

    B   hemage

    C   homage

    D   homege

11. It was just a _____ plan.

   A   perliminary

   B   preliminary

   C   prelimunary

   D   prelimonary

12. We're working in a new _____.

   A   facility

   B   fecility

   C   fucility

   D   facillity

13. Your intent was to _____ me.

   A   decieve

   B   daceive

   C   deceive

   D   dyceive

14. Please don't _____ my name on the program!

   A   misspel

   B   mispell

   C   misspell

   D   missppell

15. Their _____ were almost identical.

   A   salaries

   B   salarys

   C   salarie's

   D   saluries

16. I get sick easily; I am _____ to colds.

   A   sucseptible

   B   suceptible

   C   suseptible

   D   susceptible

17. _____ much emphasis was placed on meetings; _____ little was placed on individual work.

   A   To, too

   B   Too, too

   C   Too, to

   D   Two, too

18. The child was _____ to an eye doctor for evaluation.

   A   refered

   B   raffered

   C   referred

   D   refferred

19. Give us all the information we need including the address of your _____.

   A   residence

   B   risidence

   C   rasidence

   D   risadence

20. Because of excessive _____, we're moving to a larger room.

   A   ennrolment

   B   enrollment

   C   enrolement

   D   enrollmunt

Answer Key: Section 4, Lesson 1 (Posttest)

1. D	**2.** C	**3.** B	**4.** B	**5.** A
6. A	**7.** B	**8.** D	**9.** D	**10.** C
11. B	**12.** A	**13.** C	**14.** C	**15.** A
16. D	**17.** B	**18.** C	**19.** A	**20.** B

To ensure that you have mastered the skills in the Spelling Section:

1. Once you have checked your answers against the answer key, go back to compare your incorrect answers with the correct ones. Notice whether you understand why the answer given is the correct one. Is there a rule that explains it? Is it an exception that you can study?

2. Total your number of correct answers out of the 20 possible answers. If you had **any incorrect answers**, find the sections that explain your incorrect answers and review them carefully. If you had **fewer than 17 correct answers**, take some extra time to go back through the Spelling Section. Look at each incorrect answer throughout the chapter and go back to the corresponding lesson to see that you understand why each answer given is the correct one.

3. Before taking the TABE test, come back to review the Spelling Section. Pay special attention to areas that were difficult or confusing, but scan the entire chapter again to make sure that you feel confident in knowing and using these skills.

You have learned some of the rules but not all, and, even when you know the rules, there are always exceptions. The more you read, the more you will start to recognize when words "look right." After you have taken the posttest, review the rules and spend some time looking through the Commonly Misspelled Words list that follows 178.

Commonly Misspelled Words

Review the words that you have misspelled in the past. Try to learn 10 words at a time. Use the techniques outlined in the beginning of this section.

STUDY TIP

Many web sites offer lists of frequently misspelled words. In addition, you can find spelling lists in a large number of books on the English language. See the Appendix on page 000 for book references.

A

abnormal	aggravate	appraisal
abolition	aggressive	appreciation
abscess	aging	argument
absence	agitation	assent
accede	agreeable	assessment
accommodation	all right	assistance
accumulate	already	athletic
acknowledgment	amateur	attendance
acquaintance	amplification	attendants
acquire	analysis	attorneys
actually	analyze	attribute
adaptation	answer	audience
adequate	anticipate	auditor
adjacent	anxious	authentic
affix	apparatus	autumn
ageless	apparently	auxiliary

B

bachelor	biased	boycott
bacteria	bimonthly	briefcase
bankruptcy	biographer	bulletin
barely	bisect	bureau
basically	bombard	burglaries
believe	bondage	business
belligerent	bookkeeper	
benefited	boundary	

C

cafeteria	classified	congruent
calendar	coincidence	connoisseur
campaign	collaborate	connotation
canceled	collateral	conscience
cancellation	colonization	conscientious
candor	colossal	conscious
category	column	consensus
census	commentator	consistent
certainty	communal	consultant
challenger	computerized	continually
chameleon	concede	controller
changeable	conceive	corporal
chief	concession	correspondence
chronological	conflagration	courtesies
classification	congenial	courtesy

C

credentials	cross-reference	currency
criticism	crucial	custody

D

debtor	departure	disinterest
deceive	dependent	dispensable
decision	derogatory	disrespect
deductible	descendant	dissatisfied
de-emphasize	desert	dissimilar
defective	desperately	distasteful
defendant	dessert (food)	documentary
deferred	develop	dossier
deficit	development	drastically
definite	dilemma	durable
deliberate	disappear	dyeing
delicious	discipline	

E

economical	enthusiastic	exhibition
economy	entrepreneur	exhibitor
effects	enumerate	exhilarate
efficient	envious	existence
elaborate	enzyme	exonerate
elasticity	equipped	exorbitant
embarrass	erroneous	experiment
emergency	error	explanation
emigrant	evaluation	extension
eminent	evasive	external
emphasis	exaggerate	extraordinary
emphasize	exceed	extravagant
endorse	excel	eyeing
endurance	excitable	
enormous	exhaustible	

F

facilitation	fastener	finally
facsimile	fiendish	financial
faculties	fiery	financier
falsify	filament	fissure
familiarity	filmstrip	flecks
fascinating	finalist	flexible

F

fluorescent	foreign	forty
foliage	foresee	fourteen
forcible	forfeit	function

G

gallery	glamour	grieve
galvanized	glucose	grievous
gauge	gnash	gruesome
generalization	government	guarantee
geographic	graft	guardian
geological	grammar	guidance
ghetto	grateful	guild
glamorous	gravitational	gymnast

H

handicapped	hemoglobin	hosiery
handkerchief	hemorrhage	hostage
harass	heterogeneous	hygiene
harassment	hindrance	hygienic
height	homage	hypocrisy
helium	hors d'oeuvre	

I

idiomatic	inference	intercede
ignorant	inflammatory	interim
illegitimate	influential	intermission
illustrator	infraction	interpretive
imminent	ingenuity	interruption
immovable	inhuman	intuition
impasse	innocuous	inverted
impenetrable	innuendo	involuntary
imprisonment	innumerable	irrelevant
inasmuch as	inoculate	irreparably
incidentally	input	irrigation
indict	insurance	irritable
indispensable	integrity	itemized
individual	intelligent	itinerary

J

jealous	jovial	jurisdiction
jeopardy	judgment	justice
journal	judiciary	

K

khaki	kidney	kindergarten

L

labeled	liable	linguist
laboratory	liaison	liquefy
ladies	libel	literally
latter	liberal	logical
league	liberate	loose
leased	license	lose
legion	lien	losing
legitimate	likeness	lovable
leisure	likewise	lucrative

M

maintain	memento	mischievous
maintenance	merely	mislaid
maneuver	mileage	misspell
manual	milieu	monkeys
marital	millennium	mortgage
mechanical	miniature	movable
medieval	minuscule	muscle
mediocre	miscellaneous	

O

oceanography	omitted	outdated
offense	optional	overview
omission	ordinary	overweight

P

pamphlet	parallel	patience
panicky	parasite	patient
paradigm	pastime	peculiar

P

people's	politician	pretense
permissible	portable	previous
perseverance	possession	principal
persistent	possibilities	privilege
persuade	potato	probably
phenomenal	potatoes	procedure
phony	practically	proceed
physical	preceding	profit
physician	preferable	programmed
picnicking	preferably	promissory
pitiful	preference	pronunciation
plagiarism	preparation	pseudonym
planned	prerogative	psychiatric
playwright	presume	publicly
pneumonia	presumptuous	pursue

Q

quantities	questionnaire	quizzes
quartet	queue	

R

raisin	regrettable	resources
rarefy	reinforce	responsibility
realize	relevant	restaurant
reasonable	rendezvous	rhapsody
receipt	repetitious	rhetorical
receive	rescind	rhyme
recognizable	resemblance	rhythm
recommend	resilience	rhythmic
reconcile	resistance	

S

sacrilegious	scenes	shield
salable	schedule	siege
salaries	scissors	sieve
salient	seize	similar
satellite	separate	sincerely

S

single	stationary (fixed)	successor
skeptic	stationery (paper)	suggestion
skillful	statistics	summarize
soldier	strength	supersede
souvenir	strict	surprise
specialized	subtlety	surreptitious
specifically	subtly	surveillance
sponsor	succeed	symmetrical

T

tariff	temperament	thoughtless
taunt	temperamental	threshold
taxiing	tempt	thunderstorm
teammate	tension	tissue
technical	theater	tongue
technique	theory	totaled
technology	therefore	tragedy
telecast	thesis	transportation
telegram	thieves	traveler
telegraph	thoroughly	trembling
telescope	thought	troublemaking

U

unanimous	underweight	unmanageable
unauthorized	undoubtedly	unnecessary
unbearable	unfortunately	unusual
unconscious	uniform	unwieldy
uncovered	unify	usage
undernourished	unique	
undersea	universe	

V

vacancy	valuable	villain
vaccinate	value	vinyl
vaccination	valueless	visible
vacillate	valuing	vision
vacuum	vegetable	void
vague	vengeance	volcanoes
vain	verbal	volume
valid	verify	voluntary
valley	victory	voucher

W

warrant	width	woman's
waving	wield	women's
weather	wiring	woolly
Wednesday	withhold	worthwhile
weird	witnesses	wrapped
welfare	wives	wretched
whether	woeful	
wholly	wolves	

X

xerox	x-ray	xylophone
Xerox	X-ray	

Y

yacht	yearly	youngster
yardstick	yield	yourself
yarn	yogurt	
year	yoke	

Z

zany	zero	zodiac
zap	zest	zone
zealous	zinc	zoo

RESOURCES

English Language Reference Books

Bernstein, T. M. *The Careful Writer: A Modern Guide to English Usage.* New York: Atheneum, 1994.

Brusaw, C. T., Alred, G. J., and Oliu, W. E. *The Business Writer's Handbook.* (5th ed.) New York: St. Martin's Press, 1997.

Cazort, D. *Under the Grammar Hammer: The 25 Most Important Mistakes and How to Avoid Them.* (updated) Los Angeles: Lowell House, 1997.

Diamond, L., Fahey, M., and Diamond, H. *Executive Writing: American Style.* (2nd ed.) Berkeley, CA: Apocryphile Press, 2007.

Dutwin, P., and Diamond, H. *English The Easy Way.* (4th ed.) Hauppauge, NY: Barron's Educational Series, Inc., 2003.

Dutwin, P., and Diamond, H. *Grammar In Plain English.* (3rd ed.) Hauppauge, NY: Barron's, 1997.

Dutwin, P., and Diamond, H. *Writing The Easy Way.* (3rd ed.) Hauppauge, NY: Barron's, 2000.

Follett, W. *Modern American Usage: A Guide.* Edited and completed by Jacques Barzun and others. New York: Hill & Wang, 1998.

Goddin, N. and Palma, E. (editors) (Princeton Review). *Grammar Smart: A Guide to Perfect Usage.* New York: Villard Books, 1993.

Kipfer, B. A. (editor) *Roget's International Thesaurus* (6th ed) New York: Harper Collins, 2001.

Merriam-Webster Collegiate Dictionary. (10th ed) New York: Merriam-Webster, 1998.

Merriam-Webster Dictionary (10th ed.) 1998.

Mersand, J. and Griffith, F. *Spelling the Easy Way.* (4th ed.) Hauppauge, NY: Barron's Educational Series, Inc., 1996.

Oliu, W. E., Brusaw, C. T., and Alred, G. J. *Writing that Works.* New York: St. Martin's Press, 1980.

Sabin, W. A. *Gregg Reference Manual.* (9th ed.) New York: Glencoe McGraw-Hill, 2001.

Strunk, Jr., W. and White, E. B. *The Elements of Style.* (3rd ed.) Boston: Allyn and Bacon.

INDEX